NEWPORT COUNTY AFC

THE FIRST 100 YEARS

ANDREW TAYLOR

FOREWORD BY JOHN ALDRIDGE

AMBERLEY

ACKNOWLEDGEMENTS

This book is for all who have contributed to the story of Newport County AFC in our first 100 years. Special thanks to the many players and managers who have openly shared their memories with me over the years, to Richard Shepherd and Tony Ambrosen and all other fellow County historians who have helped preserve our unique history, and the journalists who faithfully recorded events as they happened. Photographs are courtesy of the Newport County AFC archive, the personal collections of players and staff, Ade Williams, former club photographers including Jan Preece, Duncan Jardine, Dave Smalldon, Chris Shingler, Sam Shingler, Kevin Barnes, Ashley Crowden, Ryan Hiscott and the *South Wales Argus*. If anyone has inadvertently been omitted, please contact the author via Newport County AFC.

First published 2014
This edition published 2016

Amberley Publishing
The Hill, Stroud
Gloucestershire, GL5 4EP

www.amberley-books.com

British Library Cataloguing in Publication Data.
A catalogue record for this book is available from the British Library.

ISBN 978 1 4456 6042 4 (paperback)
ISBN 978 1 4456 1819 7 (ebook)

Typesetting and Origination by Amberley Publishing.
Printed in the UK.

CONTENTS

Keith Oakes receives the Welsh Cup, 1980.

FOREWORD BY JOHN ALDRIDGE

I am a diehard Liverpool red who had the privilege of playing for the team I supported from the Kop. I had a trial in my youth, and despite scoring a hatful, didn't get the call back for fourteen years until £750,000 persuaded Oxford to part with me. I was fortunate enough to partner great players like Ian Rush and John Barnes, win all the major honours, and play for Ireland in the World Cup. It was playing for Ireland that, waiting in the tunnel to go into battle against Italy, Gianluca Vialli, one of the greatest players in the world at that time, walked past all of our big names and finally stopped toward the end of the line where I stood, and to my amazement said, 'Later, my shirt for your shirt'. It was at that point I reflected just how much I owed to Newport County! It was Newport who gave me my chance. Len Ashurst's brother, Robin, who I worked with, recommended me. £3,500 took me from south Liverpool to south Wales, and despite initial homesickness I soon settled into a club that had nothing materially, but was rich in terms of its camaraderie on and off the pitch. It was a club that had suffered years of misfortune, but was about to have its golden period when we surprised the football world by not only winning promotion and the Welsh Cup but by reaching the quarter final of the European Cup Winners' Cup! I am proud that no Football League striker has matched my overall career goals record since the war. An FA Cup Final opener is included in my total, but the one I will never forget is my first – and that was for Newport. I have deep feelings and emotions for the club. As Andrew says, the first 100 years has been a roller coaster – let's look forward to the next being just as thrilling – and a little less stressful!

INTRODUCTION

In 2012, I was asked by the Newport County AFC Supporters' Trust and Newport Museum to help with a centenary exhibition. The first request was to write up the first 100 years on five exhibition boards, with the roller-coaster highs and lows being illustrated in a maximum of 250 words per board. I responded, 'Thank goodness we have not won an awful lot!' (or words to that effect)! Thanks to Amberley Publishing, the task has been extended to 56,000 words and 150 photographs in 208 pages – still insufficient even to chart the incredible twists to the story that has been the life of this strangely wonderful – indeed unique – club.

Our history has been notably set out in words and pictures in previous publications by Richard Shepherd and Tony Ambrosen, and indeed in my two previous ventures *Look Back in Amber* and *Mission Accomplished: The Ultimate Season of Triumph*. So how could I add value in this centenary edition? The scores, the attendances and indeed the timeline are pretty well documented – and so while such detail is inescapably included, I have sought to focus a little more, where possible, on the personal anecdotes of those who were there. It has been a privilege for me, over many years, to have known and spoken to key characters in our history and in so doing, learnt far more than the detail published in the press. Countless players and managers have shared with me not only their personal memories but their emotions and funny tales from the boot camp. My only regret is that many years ago I neglected to record these, but I have done so in verbatim detail over the last decade. On every occasion I have been riveted – taken back in time and even able to soak in the atmosphere of events that passed before I was born. So what is all the fuss about? Well, here follows a quick overview of our first 100 years.

Founded in 1912, the First World War tragically stalled progress. In 1989, Newport shamefully saw its club die. In the intervening years, County had gone on to see more bad times than good. Finance was always a problem, the facilities always sub-standard. It had taken until 1939 to win promotion (from the old 3rd Division (South) to the Second Division). Even then fate was cruel. Neville Chamberlain (the Prime Minister and not the 1980s' County forward) finally stood up to Hitler, and the relevance of football would pale to insignificance, as the young of the country would once more perish during another six years of world war. By the time we reassembled, the best that we could do was to field a makeshift team of veterans and local youngsters. Nevertheless, at long last we took our place in the Second Division, and set about putting the club in the record books – unfortunately for all the wrong reasons, with 133 goals conceded, including a 13-0 defeat at Newcastle! We were mercilessly put back in our place and, apart from briefly threatening in 1982/83, were never to return to the second tier. Indeed, we were not too slow in joining the 4th Division, formed in 1958/59. From 1962/63, the new basement of the Football League was to be our home for many years, flirting more with re-election than promotion. The 1970s started with a serious attempt at a new record, i.e. the most games from the beginning of the season before claiming a League victory!

In 1972/73, however, the form book was turned on its head. Even then, fate would display a cruel sense of humour. A last-day victory at home to Bury, added to a combination of other results, would see us deservedly promoted again at last. In those days, we kicked off fifteen minutes later than most other clubs so the ground was buzzing with score updates. The tension spread to the players, who were being kept informed by hundreds of transistor radios clutched to eager ears. Action at Somerton became frantic, but at 3-1 up we looked good. A BBC radio announcer then reported that Crewe had unbelievably beaten high flying Hereford 1-0, in what was the least likely result of the day that could have gone our way. The scenes were chaotic. The excitement spread to the players, who inevitably lost concentration, and with six minutes remaining, Bury pulled a goal back. Just two minutes later County scored again only to fail to keep the Shakers out at the other end with two minutes to go. 4-3 – what a game! The whistle blew. 'Keeper John Macey did a somersault. Most fans had no idea what to do. As a twelve-year-old living in Cwmbran, the choice was made for me. Alan

Hughes grabbed my arm, and dashed to the car to beat the traffic. So clearly do I remember driving on the outskirts of Ringland with periods of silent disbelief interrupted by unbridled screams of celebration, and a few words that would have seen me grounded for a week!

Looking back, why did we not realise? This was Newport County, our club! How could good fortune smile on us? Without any apology or thought to the consequences in this corner of Wales, the BBC presenter read out a summary of the day, explaining that Newport would have to wait until the following Friday, and the result of Stockport versus promotion rivals Aldershot. Crewe had not beaten Hereford. Of course they hadn't. Had we stopped to realise this was the County, then we would have known that it was fate having a laugh again at our expense. Far more believable that the impeccable mother of broadcasting, the BBC, had earlier contrived to get the score wrong! No point really asking how Aldershot fared the following week at Edgeley Park is there. The Shots were our bogey side, although we had miraculously completed the 'double' over them that season. A 1-1 draw saw them take our rightful place by a fractional goal average difference of 0.12. Within four seasons we nearly went bankrupt. The arrival of Colin Addison led us to the Great Escape, saving us and condemning Workington to non-League wilderness.

Then it all got so much better. Forever known as 'The Season of Triumph', 1979/80 not only saw promotion clinched with a sensational last-day win at Championship-chasing Walsall, but a Second Division scalp was claimed in the shape of Shrewsbury, winning both legs and lifting the Welsh Cup for the first time in the club's history (did I gloss over the only previous occasion we reached the final in 1963, just to lose to a village team called Borough United?). This meant a venture into Europe, and suddenly our unfashionable little club had the football world enthralled, holding what seemed the entire East German national side in the form of Carl Zeiss Jena, to a 2-2 first leg draw behind the Iron Curtain, before sliding out 1-0 in front of a packed, disbelieving Somerton Park in one of the most one-sided, unjust, games you could ever see. Efforts off (or indeed over) the line, a rattled crossbar and a late wonder save to deny captain Keith Oakes, could not cancel out one of their few attempts. With the iconic Tommy Tynan's two away goals counting double, we were that close to being in the semi-final of the European Cup Winners' Cup. 1982/83 saw certain promotion spurned with a disastrous late run of form, and never again would we come so close. Indeed, that side would soon break up, including the sale of the prolific John Aldridge and Tynan for ludicrously small fees and no sell-on clauses. Aldridge went on to international fame and glory. County, need you ask, were in the Vauxhall Conference and bankrupt before the decade was out. It is hard to describe the pain of losing your football club. To their eternal credit, County fans would not lie down. A new club was created, firstly called Newport AFC and then, in 1999, reverting to Newport County AFC, with the aim to restore League football. The new club has not had it easy, twice being exiled across the border fighting for the right to play in the football pyramid.

The impact of exile cannot be overstated – and neither can the demands placed on board members and the amber army of volunteers, who kept us going in the most difficult times when the ambition, initially summed up by our slogan 'Football with A Future', appeared to be a forlorn hope. But the last few years have made it so worthwhile. Dean Holdsworth's team in 2009/10 set records, when they won promotion back to the Conference. Justin Edinburgh came in and inspired not only a successful relegation battle but a first ever trip to Wembley in 2011/12 for the FA Trophy final. We lost, and wondered if we would ever be back. A celebrating York fan came up to me in the car park after the game and said with conviction, 'Don't worry – you will be back here again next season and go up!' As if! The board made the most important decision since going back into exile by moving to Rodney Parade. One hundred years previous, we had been formed as an alternative to the rugby code. Could this, the famous home of Newport rugby, ironically be the place that would see us enjoy our greatest success – in our centenary year? Surely that would be too farfetched, even for our 'unique' little club. I hope you enjoy the journey of our first 100 years.

Andrew Taylor
Newport County AFC Club Historian
and Secretary of the Former Players' Association

1

THE EARLY YEARS

There had been abortive earlier attempts to set up a football club to represent Newport but by 1912, thanks to steelworkers who had moved from the Midlands, there was an increase in popularity of the round ball game in a region dominated by rugby. And so it was that our story – or should we say Greek tragedy – begins. Originally called Newport & Monmouth County AFC, the team secured a ground at Somerton Park, close to Lysaght's steelworks. The black and amber strip of both the Newport rugby and Wolverhampton Wanderers clubs was adopted, and from a supporters' competition in 1913, the club nickname the 'Ironsides' was chosen. How little could they have appreciated the dramatic impact of their actions on generations of future supporters. Writing in 1939, one at that first meeting at the Tredegar Arms admitted, 'I don't think any of us full realised just what anxieties and difficulties lay ahead.' Shortly before the club was founded, the *Titanic* was launched, with tragic consequences. The difference with County is that the *Titanic* only went down once.

Shares were issued at 10s each and former Celtic star Davy McDougall was appointed player-manager in July. As a sign of things to come, the Welsh League executive expressed surprise that County had not applied to join – instead opting for the Second Division of the Southern League. More than 100 applications were received to play for the club, and at a board meeting ten were accepted with the club saying, 'They include some well-known men, but it is thought advisable not to mention their names until they have signed on.' McDougall did not have to contend with website message-board rumours, although talk was rife and trial matches were organised in August, with proceeds going to the hospital and charity. Ambitious plans were also being made for the ground with expectations of big crowds to be accommodated. Supervising the work was Bert Moss, a local referee and builder, already writing his name into County folklore and described by the press as there being, 'no more wholehearted supporter of the new club, or wholehearted devotee of the dribbling code.' The lavish descriptions of the ground were 'Jerry Shermanesque', and actually consisted of tipping and banking hundreds of loads of rubbish. A large wooden hut was built in the corner to house dressing rooms, a plunge bath and a small office, and three members of the press could squeeze into a wooden box at the side of the pitch. Over 2,000 were estimated to have been at the first trial game – impressive, but a long way short of one press report that accommodation would eventually provide for '65,000 persons'. The only undiscovered talent trying out was local boy George Groves. He would make his own contribution to County – apart from scoring twice for the 'Black and Whites' against the 'Black and Ambers' – as in future years his son, a certain Billy Lucas, would make an impression with County, but more of him later. County's first game was a friendly at Risca to open their new ground on 2 September 1912.

A 1-0 defeat of Risca (sadly no one thought at the time to record the scorer's name) had supporters looking forward to County's debut in the Southern League Division 2, in five days' time on 7 September at Mid-Rhondda. A crowd of around 5,000 witnessed history with a number of County firsts. Actually, there were only around 2,000 in the ground at kick-off, and it swelled as the game went on – the opposite of many games in future years when the terraces would become noticeably sparser as the game progressed. The first toss for kick-off was lost. Scottish forward George Fife became the first County goalscorer, following brilliant work by young right-winger Andy Holt, who claimed the first assist. Davy McDougall scored the first ever County penalty and the hastily assembled Mid-Rhondda side, who had been struggling to field a team, saw their right half Thomas become the first opponent dismissed when he clashed with Enoch Westwood. He also had the ignominious status of being the first victim of terrace boo-boys. In later years, it would become traditional for the unfortunate player to patrol the right wing to feel the wrath of impatient fans – but Holt's impressive form meant they instead had to pick on the recipient of his fine crosses, centre forward Bob Vowles, who had a miserable time even though he had the comfort of adding the third and final goal. Described as 'being rather weak', that was to be his only score before leaving after Christmas, having failed to change opinions in five different positions.

The Supporters' Club Committee in August 1912, at the King of Prussia near Somerton Park.

The historic first line-up assume their playing formation, with 'keeper and full backs standing and forwards in the front, a few days before the Risca game. *From left (back row)*: George Perry, Dave Ewings, Ted Husbands. Dick Williams, Billy Taylor, Fred Good. *Middle*: Andy Holt, Proctor Hall, Bob Vowles, George Fyfe, Enoch Westwood, Fred Good Jnr. *Front*: Albert Cox, Tommy Thornton, Davy McDougall.

The score had masked a less than scintillating first half, but there was great excitement for the next game, evidenced by the 1,000-strong County following that made the short trip to Ninian Park for the first encounter with Cardiff City. Meanwhile, Cardiff had to play Mid-Rhondda and, despite winning 1-0, made harder work of it than County. So with the team unchanged, there was optimism – a word sometimes used but rarely believed over the next century.

A phrase that would remain in vogue was the headline used by journalist Pivot, following the game; 'A Tale of Hard Luck' he wrote as Tommy Thornton became the first player unable to continue the game through injury – and after only five minutes. Cardiff were restricted to a 2-0 win, both scored in the twenty minutes following Thornton's withdrawal, and with McDougall hastily rearranging his side. For the second game running, the dependable Ted Husbands, who already possessed three Welsh Cup Winner's medals, was in defiant form in goal.

The first Welsh League fixture was played two days later on 16 September, at Pontypridd – County lost 2-1, though Proctor Hall netted another first. The third Southern League fixture was a 1-0 home defeat to Swansea Town, but is more memorable as another example of either the state of public transport, the inability of local football fans to tell the time, or the clash with shift hours, with the 3,000 crowd at kick-off having swelled again to around 5,000 by half-time. The latter, little wonder in later years, traditional 3 p.m. kick-off time was put back fifteen minutes. Inevitably, that game saw another first for the fledgling club – this time the first referee to suffer the wrath of an angry County crowd. The press reported: 'A couple of policemen marked the progress of the referee to the dressing room. The crowd surged round him, but beyond venting their feelings by lung exercise there was no attempt to interfere with Mr. Osbourne's comfort.' County were hauled before the League, and the following Tuesday the club was fined half a guinea, but not for failing to control the crowd – right back Perry (who later became the first to score an own goal) was unregistered.

Early performances were generally uninspiring – one reporter commenting typically that 'The second was as dull as the first half.' Attendance remained consistent, although only 2,000 (perhaps they stopped counting after kick-off) witnessed the first English side to appear at Somerton when Southern League Division 1 side Portsmouth visited for a friendly on 3 October and left Wales with a 3-2 win. A few days later, County were before the management committee again, and handing over money they could ill afford – this time ordered to pay £10 to Brentford for the transfer of left-sided player David Ewing who, after fourteen appearances, was seen no more and perhaps can claim the title of first expensive flop.

Mardy became the first ever cup opponents – County triumphant thanks to George Fyfe in the first preliminary round of the Welsh Cup. Performances were improving, and Swansea made an eagerly anticipated early return. The Swans made no mistake after a 1-1 draw and won the replay 4-1. By the end of October, Pivot assuaged the disappointment of that result by reporting excitedly that they were signing Wolves' Welsh amateur international, Ernie Hammett, who had been a teacher at Eveswell School. As it turned out, the talented Hammett, who also played for Wales against England at Lawn Tennis, did not make his debut until the end of December and, having been captain until the war, failed to rejoin. Instead, Ernie took up rugby and became an England international.

Before then saw a game which certainly divided opinion among both sets of fans. A 1-1 draw at Aberdare Athletic in the second preliminary round of the Welsh Cup saw an enthralling replay, with Aberdare leading 4-3 during half an hour of extra time, having finished 3-3 at ninety minutes. With just five minutes remaining, the light had faded so badly that the referee decided to set yet another County first and abandoned the game. It only delayed matters, as the next game, played at Aberdare, saw County fall victim to their hosts' frustrations, losing 4-0.

Having been pulled up a couple of times already by the Southern League, County were soon on the receiving end of a decision of the Welsh League management committee. In November, Cwm argued successfully that their 3-0 defeat at Somerton should be declared a friendly and not a League fixture. On 12 December, Durham of Argoed became the first to score an own goal for County in the Monmouthshire Senior Cup.

Christmas games are, of course, a traditional feast for fans, who immediately look in hope of a tasty derby when the fixtures are published. County's first was at Southend. An overnight stay did not prepare them as they lost 1-0. Perhaps they had a bad night, as neither were they showing festive goodwill, as Southend played seventy-five minutes with ten men and at one stage had only eight on the field. It was described as 'one of the roughest ever seen on the Southend ground'. The reporter added: 'The referee quite lost his control of the players and at one time it seemed the match would develop into a free fight and the crowd threatened to break onto the ground. Wileman of Southend had his collar bone broken and Thomason and Wilson had to be carried off. The crowd hooted the Newport players loudly.' County's players, while subsequently admitting that some of the exchanges had been vigorous, rejected the complaints. 4 January should have seen the first visit of an English club, Croydon Common, for a League game and there was not just disappointment but a big financial setback as that morning's heavy rain saw it cancelled, with the loss of a gate expected to reach 8,000. By the time the game with Mardy on 11 January was postponed, there was cause for concern; this was the fourth match lost to weather, meaning that since November gate income had been no more than £25. Lysaght's became involved, and various fundraisers were held, including a sports day with very significant cash prizes arranged for Whitsun. And then County were hauled before the Committee again and fined a guinea for fielding an ineligible player.

Second-placed Luton, who had only lost once all season, became the first English side to visit for a competitive game, inspiring County's best performance to date with a 5-1 win. Although the Hatters had not been helped by having to go straight from the railway station to the pitch, County were in impressive form, and little could be taken away from them.

Relationships with Southend did not improve in the return. Financial difficulties, with another 5,000 crowd expected, were seriously compounded when the Shrimpers, who by now were showing a rather timid disposition, persuaded the referee to cancel it, claiming that the fine ashes spread to help dry the surface made it too dangerous. When the rumour went around that the referee had declared it unfit, most thought it was a joke. Then a Southend official came out and asked for the train timetable; when he was told that there was one to London at 5.20 p.m., the team left the grounf two minutes later. County's claims that the Southend pitch on Christmas Day had been in worse condition, a match that gave Southend a more than healthy £850 gate, fell on deaf ears. To prove the point, players and others entertained the crowd with six-a-side games. In March, top scorer Andy Holt, who had played in all but one of the forty-one games to date, became the first player sold to Cardiff for £100 and an agreement to play a friendly. But a slice was taken when the League ordered payment of £15 expenses to Southend. George Fyfe was also then transferred to Swansea, who had missed out on Holt for an undisclosed, fairly substantial fee. Already County were forced to be a selling club. Cardiff caused upset by resting most of their stars when playing the fundraiser at Easter, including Holt. In early April, tensions were running high with the Monmouthshire County FA, with a number of complaints flying back and forth aired at a meeting at offices in Skinner Street, and County accused of 'mudslinging'. At the same meeting,

County complained Risca had used an ineligible player in the semi-final of the Monmouthshire Senior Cup, but the protest was ruled out of order.

Bert Moss had been a familiar figure in the town throughout the season, hurrying around raising funds for the following day's away game, but the first year ended with County £700 in debt. The annual meeting at The King focused on the potential to raise funds through Lysaght's employees buying shares, and the need to improve the ground ready for the next season. The meeting was enthusiastic and a further 200 shares were bought on the day. McDougall was re-engaged as secretary-manager, but left to become steward of the Excelsior Club.

Sam Hollis was appointed manager, bringing his ever-present bowler and gold watch over from Bristol City, where he had been the go-to man every time they needed someone to step into the breach. Hollis was insistent upon a stand being built on the side that many years later became famous as 'Paddy's Bar' and this was completed just after the start of the season. Given the number of games cancelled, it was crucial that the pitch was improved and the league complimented County on their efforts. An almost entirely new squad was assembled, and admission gained to the Southern Alliance, comprising First and Second Division clubs for midweek games. This meant withdrawing from the Welsh League – and yet another fine of

Glasgow-born Louis Lean had been a goalscoring centre forward for Liverpool's reserves and, while perhaps overweight, had an outstanding season fulfilling a number of positions, mainly in defence.

£50, reduced on appeal to £25. This competition provided the opening game of the 1913/14 season, and a 1-0 win at Cardiff, despite the players running from the station to the ground while carrying their own kit – a new look of amber and black stripes and white shorts. County's first ever FA Cup tie was played on 27 September, with Mond Nickel Works from Swansea showing little metal in the first qualifying round as County progressed 6-1. Matthews scored County's first hat-trick, although some records credit one of the goals to Frank Lindley. To make sure of his place in the record books, veteran former Aston Villa star Billy Matthews duly scored another hat-trick in the next round in an identical score against Cardiff Corries. The third qualifying round was the pinnacle as County lost a replay at Aberdare.

Hollis, who later found himself censured for poaching players from Caerleon, then pulled off a real coup, signing Irish International Joe Enright from Leeds City for £50 – a whole fiver more than the rest of the team put together! Hollis had already signed Fred Flanders from Derby – how little could anyone have realised that in a short time his surname would be forever associated with the battleground that saw some of the greatest losses during the First World War. Before then, in more innocent times, crowds were up and thankfully income was on the increase, and the December game with Luton saw a record 12,000 attendance. However, despite Lysaght's generosity, the bottom line of the balance sheet remained a huge concern, especially after the costs of the ground's works was taken into account. Worse was to come with demands being made to pay off transfer fees by 31 March, with a further £65 by 11 April. It may have helped if County could have avoided so many fines. In November, they had been penalised by a guinea for playing an unregistered player in the Alliance, and at the same meeting five guineas for playing a weakened team against Croydon. A public meeting in January saw the necessary response, and early liquidation was avoided. Injuries had proven problematic, and rugby stars Herbie Wreford and Reg Plummer helped out by playing with unfamiliar-shaped balls. Hollis had not learnt his lesson, and Caerleon were in no mood for apologies when, for the second time, there was a claim of poaching one of their players, after Payne failed to show for their game, only for them to then discover he had played for County the day before! Bert Moss this time sent an open letter to the Editor of the *Argus* pointing out the ambiguities of the rules of the various leagues. The League hearing adjourned the case for written evidence; Hollis claimed he had been away all day and not had time to go home to bring it. When reconvened, it was clear that permission had been given for one game only and County lost the argument on the interpretation of Rule 26. Bearing in mind the perilous financial position, the fine was kept at £2.

In April, County's star signing Enright made the headlines for all the wrong reasons. He was summoned for being drunk and disorderly in Skinner Street and pleaded to not being drunk but being 'disorderly under provocation', for which he was 'very sorry'. The incident at 11.35 p.m. on a Sunday night had seen the small and slight Enright, who was hardly built for it, in a fight with another who had called him an 'opprobrious name'. Despite the police officer saying he was 'crying drunk', he claimed he had only partaken of two small bottles of stout. The judge was unconvinced and fined him 10s 6d or to serve fourteen days. He was then literally sent to Coventry, signing for them at the end of the season and freeing up some cash, as he was the first player on the maximum £4 wage. Of all Hollis' signings, it was 'keeper Bob McLeod, signed from Raith Rovers, who had more than justified his reputation with some outstanding displays, including saving two penalties at Luton. Unfortunately, he moved on at the end of the season to QPR, but could be thankful there was no YouTube in those days to preserve every indiscretion, as at Croydon he 'ankle tapped' a ball boy in frustration.

Results had been good, with only two defeats in the last sixteen Southern League games, a sixth place finish, and gate receipts had been double the previous season; and so it was felt to sustain support to build on this for the next season. Despite some very rocky financial problems, things were actually looking very promising. The early struggles had been worth it and surely from here it would be onwards and upwards ... after all, what could go wrong now?

Inability to pay summer wages meant that the team was weakened; only Flanders was retained and only a handful, apart from local players, chose to return for the 1914/15 campaign. That was a minor concern, and indeed football itself was rendered an irrelevance as Britain declared war on Germany on 4 August. Midweek football was abandoned and attendances dropped. The season was completed, and frustratingly a record 13-0 Boxing Day win over Abertillery was expunged when they resigned from the league. A record 10-1 defeat was suffered at Coventry, with a clearly sober Enright sinking four. By the end of the season, only local amateurs were left. From the outset of war, there had been great debate about the appropriateness of organised football continuing, but the decision was finally taken that it be suspended and replaced by friendlies and local wartime leagues, as by then the true horrors of war had really hit home. Bob Hammett, who had made his debut in the final game of 1913/14, was killed in action on 25 September 1916. Alfred Edwards was wounded on 22 October 1916, but returned to the front, and was tragically killed in action a week before the Armistice was signed.

County struggled on manfully, endeavouring to keep a presence ready for the resumption of normality – whenever that would be. In November 1917, they gave up the ghost after a 0-0 home draw with Barry. The Company of Newport and Monmouth County was wound up.

Or was it? Bert Moss in particular had been very active, making the most of playing after 1915 at venues such as the Dell and Ashton Gate, with lobbying activities that were to pay off when normality was finally resumed!

NEWPORT COUNTY'S PROGRAMME
Newport County A.F.C. made a successful commencement on Monday when they opened the Risca club's new ground. The visitors, who were not fully represented, won by a goal to nil.
On fixture lists which have been published the County are down to entertain either Wolverhampton Wanderers or on Pentre with a friendly to-morrow (Thursday), but this is an error, and the home season commences next Saturday with a Southern League fixture against Mid-Rhondda.

Left: A press cutting from the first ever game in 1912.

Below: The Supporters' Club in 1914.

The County side that won at Cardiff City 1-0 in the Southern Alliance, 3 September 1913.

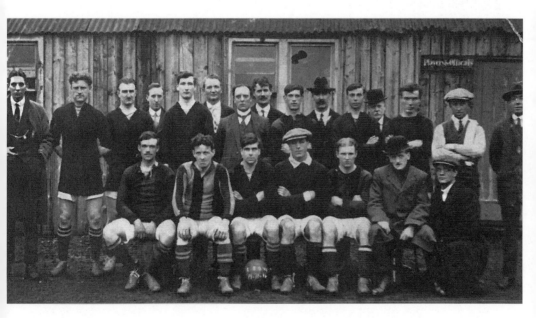

In the midst of war, County line up outside the Somerton Park dressing rooms, 19 October 1916. First season 'keeper Ted Husbands, wearing his cap, sits in the front row.

2

WAR IS OVER – THE FIGHT BEGINS

In November 1918, the nation breathed a sigh of relief and began to wonder how the savagery of the previous four years could be put behind them. Could family lives be returned to some semblance of normality when so many had suffered such tragic personal loss? Bill Shankly was famously quoted as saying: 'Some people believe football is a matter of life and death, I am very disappointed with that attitude. I can assure you it is much, much more important than that.' Even he would not have ventured that comment in 1918, but the reality was that to return to normality – whatever that was – there would be a need for people to gather and find enjoyment, enthrallment and some kind of escape from everyday lives. And so it was that organised football – the working man's game – became an integral part of the road to recovery.

Thanks to Bert Moss and company, the name of Newport County was sufficiently in the public consciousness to arrange a series of friendlies. There had been a one-off game with Caerleon in 1917, but the first post-war game was enjoyed by 3,000 on Christmas morning as County beat Cardiff 2-1, although the return the next day was lost 3-0. There were some familiar names for fans to cheer, such as Husbands, Flanders, Groves and Lean, and a clutch of new local amateurs had their chance to stake their claim.

There was an issue to be addressed as the freehold owners of Somerton Park had sold it on and, with the lease due to expire in June 1919, the new owners were looking for a significant rent increase. W. R. Lysaght eventually came to the rescue, and bought Somerton for £2,200 for his employees, who promptly formed a committee and let it to County. While supporters and players were just happy to be out there again, behind the scenes, club directors across the land were scrambling for places in the reorganised leagues. Football has always been highly politicised, and one can only imagine the endless discussions and deals that must have taken place. The press were easily able to fill column inches with the latest speculation. County applied to the League it had been in before, although it was anticipated to be weaker than previously. On 5 February 1919, it was resolved that the First Division be increased to twenty-two clubs. There was heated argument, with provincial sides claiming they had been discriminated against and a protracted discussion on the future of the Welsh clubs. The suggestion was actually made that English clubs should not be forced to travel to Wales, and 'the Welsh clubs should play football among themselves for one year of reconstruction with the right of promotion afterwards and with the right to apply for any vacancy that might occur'. This was greeted as being the death blow for football in Wales, and it was agreed that the management committee should meet a deputation of clubs in Cardiff.

County were unabashed, and lobbying continued to take a place in the extended First Division, with one source claiming they stood 'a sparkling chance', particularly that concerns over inaccessibility difficulties and associated extra costs for clubs travelling did not apply to the same extent as it would when playing other Welsh clubs. It did not say much for locals though, or that Moss relied on the support of relative newcomers, when, in an appeal to the League, he made the point that, 'We have a great crowd of Midland people who have been cradled in Association football who will gather around us.' He added, 'I may also point out that the Great Western Railway Company have proposed to erect a station near our grounds at Somerton Park.' Meetings in Cardiff and Manchester followed, with a plethora of suggestions put forward. Press speculation mounted regarding County's chances of actually being elected to the First Division. On-field performances would be far from sufficient to stake a claim, but would at least help, though performances were variable to say the least. Western Cavalry Depot were forced to retreat with an 11-3 hiding, with Billy Richards scoring five, but five of the next six games were lost, and seven goals were conceded against Cardiff. Before then, however, 3 April was the day the tireless lobbying efforts would be tested. When the results were announced it was Swansea, Brentford, Gillingham and Merthyr who were elected, with County following just six votes behind. Moss was disappointed, and cited a change in procedure which allowed the Second Division clubs to vote as being the reason for missing out. It was understood that Merthyr's previous higher standing in the table had made them 'entitled to go up'. Best hopes rested in that the position was likely to be reviewed in 1920/21 – Moss was as determined as ever. Surely some good fortune had to come County's way at some stage. Then on 3 June 1919 came the press headline 'Southern League Div 1 – Newport County Promoted', and they hadn't even kicked a ball! Stalybridge Celtic had resigned. Suddenly, the fixture list made exciting reading, with names such as Norwich, Plymouth, QPR, Southampton, Portsmouth and Cardiff being in stark contrast to the far weaker Second Division. Had Stalybridge Celtic's travelling costs not forced them to seek a place in the Central League, you may well question if you would be reading this book today.

Bert Moss was kept busy over Whitsun by considering applicants for the secretary-manager's job. The news had prompted forty-seven applications and the successful candidate was Harry Parkes, once with West Bromwich and now assistant manager at Coventry. A new company was formed with a proposal to raise £4,000 by selling 5s shares, and a 'meet the manager' session was no doubt welcomed – but a little less so after a report that the new colours would be blue and white. The Supporters' Club was reinvigorated, with membership soon reaching 300, and cash pledges and fundraising ideas put forward. In 1989, the slogan 'Football With A Future' was adopted, and in 1919 marketing was also the order of the day, with the message 'All Roads Lead to Somerton Park'. Parkes made encouraging new signings, including George Grove, Ted 'Whiskey' Jones and Wolves pair Pat Collins and Arthur Brookes. Fred Good continued as trainer. The popular Ernie Hammett wrote to Moss saying that 'I shall only be too delighted to try my hand again.' However, this did not transpire and he went on to international rugby fame.

Another due to return was one of the most popular pre-war players, Fred Flanders. Parkes may have been forgiven for struggling to put aside any personal jealousy of the robust full-back, as had Flanders not taken the honour of being the youngest player to appear in an FA Cup Final, the honour would have rested with the manager! For some reason, Flanders instead signed for Mansfield. Parkes' mind was no doubt taken up with other concerns – namely where his new signings would live. There was a serious shortage of accommodation in Newport and this was to prove a problem throughout the season as players were having to make long journeys, particularly from the Midlands. A crowd of 3,000 watched the trial game, and there were great hopes having seen the talent on offer of the dawning of a new era.

The season kicked off at Norwich, not in blue and white but claret and blue stripes, and they returned home on the receiving end of a 4-1 walloping. Norwich kicked off playing uphill with the sun in their faces – and for County

Given previous encounters, Southend were probably nervous when visiting to play this County side on 8 September 1919 – the kit had been borrowed from West Bromwich Albion.

Shares deposit receipt dated 5 August 1920, signed by Harry Parkes across the stamps.

much of the season was to remain downhill, with few opportunities to shine. In October, the familiar amber and black returned for a match at top of the table QPR, to supporters' chants of 'Here We Go Again!' County were unlucky to lose to a last-minute goal. Indeed, they tended to do well against the top sides, but League performances were patchy, apart from an FA Cup run which saw three qualifying rounds lead to a first-round tie at home to Leicester, and a 2-0 replay defeat in front of 21,000. County's history is littered with 'what if County won cup games', and this was the first – the next round would have seen them play Chelsea and presented to George V.

It had taken seven games to record the first League win – at home to Plymouth – and the commutes for players proved far from helpful. The board finally lost their patience when five missed their train connection, meaning that the 3-0 defeat for the return at Plymouth saw the spectacle of Parkes in goal for the first time in his life, trainer Fred Good understandably not living up to his surname, and the laughable sight of a Plymouth amateur F. W. Worden making his way from the crowd to make up the numbers. It was decided that for the following season all players would have to live locally. You had to feel sorry for Jimmy Hindmarsh – the future manager signed in time to play against Watford and made the eighteen-hour journey from the north-east, only to miss the game fast asleep in the dressing room.

One commuter was Nottingham-based eccentric 'keeper Jack Cooper, whose real name was John Holloway. He produced some heroics during the season, but did little to justify his nickname of 'Genial Jack Cooper' when appearing in the dock in November accused of maliciously wounding a man by striking him on the head with a sharp instrument and rendering him unconscious for twenty-four hours. Cooper was granted bail in order to play against Swindon. Perhaps reports of his temper almost frightened the crowd away as there were only 500 in the ground fifteen minutes before kick-off – although the final attendance was just under 4,000. Jack went on to give a wonderful display in a 2-0 win. A few days later, the complainant admitted to having a long-standing grievance with Cooper's brother and with no evidence as to who had struck the blow the charge, which had been reduced from malicious assault to common assault, was dismissed. Attendances generally remained strong and despite the eighteenth-placed finish, a record crowd of 10,371 saw Billy Gaughan's effort defeat Champions Portsmouth in the final game. An unusual upright runner, he was a wonderful dribbler, but never headed the ball as he was said to have a surgical plate in his head.

County had received good news in March, when it was announced that they, as one of the five clubs needing to reapply, had secured their place in the League for the following season. Far better was to come on 31 May 1920, when it was decided at the Football League AGM that the Southern League First Division would become the Third Division of the Football League. What a debt of gratitude was owed to Stalybridge.

The insistence on living local meant that County had to do without the services of Jackie Mann and captain Pat Collins, who was another to have played in an FA Cup final. Collins was a real loss; his presence being coolness personified as he smiled his way effortlessly through games. Supporters did not have long to grieve their departure as an influx of newcomers arrived, nearly all of who were of 'biggish build', rectifying a literal weakness in the previous season's side. The press had also reported the signing of Aston Villa's Clem Stephenson, who later captained Huddersfield to three successive League Championships, and the renowned England international Harry Hampton, who would eventually join but not until 1922. It traspired that the press had fallen for a prank, with a joker having obtained Somerton Park headed notepaper to pass them this scoop! In reality, Sammy Blott signed from Plymouth for £225, and that was dwarfed by the £400 fee for Merthyr's centre half back William Chivers. Sadly, he was never to appear; shortly later having a nervous breakdown, although he did turn out subsequently in the probables v. possibles trial match. Yet another FA Cup final star also joined the ranks – Chelsea's Andy Walker.

The fixture list was arranged so that sides would play each other at home and then away on successive Saturdays, although the openers against Reading and Bristol Rovers were interspersed. A law change was also introduced so that you could not be offside from a throw in. Before then, the first AGM reported a deficit on the previous season of just over £638.

Parkes reported among laughter that he was more confident and was in a better position than the previous year, when he had a matter of weeks to put a team together for £150. That shareholders' meeting was followed on by a town meeting, when more laughter came in response to a comment about County's female supporters by Raymond Gibbs that, 'Another valuable asset has been the support in good weather or bad, from the ladies. They have even gone loyally to visiting matches – sometimes too without their husbands!'

The players were taken on a trip around the Wye Valley in a charabanc and taxis with a 'sumptuous tea' at Tintern four days before the first ever League game – at home against Reading on 28 August. A record 14,500 crowd saw an unfortunate 1-0 defeat thanks to an outstanding series of saves by the visiting 'keeper. Despite the result, there was great optimism; this quickly faded as the next four were also lost. Perhaps the signs were there in the 3-2 loss in the first League away game at Bristol Rovers. The popular and dependable Cooper somehow conspired to throw the ball through his own legs into his own net. Arthur Wolstenholme scored the first ever League goal after Walker drew the defence before slipping it to him and then placing it neatly in the corner of the net. Walker himself scored the second, becoming the first to score a League penalty for the club. The first League win did not come until 25 September at Exeter, thanks again to Wolstenhome with a top-corner shot, which was a week after the first point had been obtained with no score at home to Plymouth. Cooper was up to his tricks at Millwall. Early in the second half, 20,000 vociferous home fans were giving him their traditional welcome, including throwing missiles, some of which had hit their target. He turned to see one 'fan' aiming to throw a bottle, and so decided to take matters into his own hands. The press reports include: 'He left his charge and went into the barracking crowd but he was promptly thrown back.' Another added: 'He stood it as long as he could and then to the surprise of everybody, he climbed over the fence and argued the matter out with his tormentors. His incursion into the spectators' quarters was followed by his rapid expulsion back again to the sward'. Millwall were punished with a fortnight's ground closure, and Cooper was later severely cautioned by the Welsh FA for 'not being discreet in retaliating to the crowd'.

A new attendance record was set in November for the FA Cup visit of Merthyr; 15,000 watched the 0-0 draw. The evening before had seen Bert Moss's unselfish work rewarded by a testimonial dinner, at which he was awarded an inscribed gold watch and a wallet of treasury notes. An injury-hit side lost the replay 4-0. Injuries were really taking their toll as the season progressed, and just before Christmas an unnamed club official wrote to the *Argus* pointing out the damaging effect of complaints and rumours, stating, 'There are people who think that it is an easy task to direct the affairs of a senior football club. This may be true of clubs who are earning many League points and greatly improving their financial standing, but it is quite a different matter when a club suffers defeats, when players are crocked and poor, nay, rotten gates are the reward.' Truth be told, County had not been fulfilling the terms of their lease on the ground, and some difficult meetings were held with the Lysaght's Works Committee. At least this resulted in a lease being granted, which meant that a stumbling block to further improvements was resolved and a financial crisis was averted.

The other incident of note in this season was a return to Mid-Rhondda for a South Wales Cup replay. Though County fielded mainly reserves, this game was remarkable for the scenes that surrounded the home crowds' desire to express their opinions to the referee on the final whistle. (At least that had been his whistle – an idiot in the crowd had blown every time County attacked and did so at the precise instant a goal-bound shot was on its way from County's Shelton. The goal stood.) Mr Prince of Blackwood was struck several times despite the players, officials and police forming a guard to usher him from the pitch while taking blows themselves. One supporter stated in all seriousness that had the referee not been dragged away, he would have been murdered. And to think he had been a late replacement for an official from Hereford. 1,000 angry fans remained for over an hour, and also threatened County's directors, accusing them of having bribed the official. And so it was that Mid-Rhondda became the second club to have their ground closed after a visit by the boys from Newport.

In April, County won their first silverware – the reserves beat Ebbw Vale 1-0 at Somerton Park to lift the Monmouthshire Senior Cup. Injuries meant that Parkes had to step out of retirement, although he was one of the star performers on the day. A great solo effort from Jimmy Gittins, who ran half the length of the pitch and sent in a crashing shot from 20 yards, ultimately decided the game. County finished fifteenth, unbeaten in their last six games, but the reserves were actually a financial drain, and Cardiff visited for an end-of-season fundraiser raising £300 with reduced admission prices, a game that County won 1-0 in front of 11,000.

The 1921/22 campaign saw Flanders finally return, but it was a relatively settled squad; the most significant change happened at boardroom level, where Moss stepped down as chairman to be replaced by Cllr J. S. Johnson, although he remained an active director. Walker had considered moving to the United States, but decided to stay and was made captain. He also caused much comment when at home against Bristol Rovers, where County lost 1-0. He appeared to deliberately miss a penalty that had been awarded after an opponent caught the ball, having mistakenly believed that the whistle had blown. A reporter claimed that Walker admitted after the game that he missed on purpose, and commended his chivalry. Moss and Walker complained, and the paper was forced to print a retraction; his actual words after the game having been 'I tried to place it.' It was a disappointing season though, with thirteen games being lost by only the odd goal, and re-election was narrowly escaped on goal average; although a 5-0 defeat at Southampton in the last game threatened that advantage over next-placed Exeter. Although the League gave little joy, fans' interests were maintained with a memorable FA Cup run.

1921/22 and County are now a Football League club – seen here before a 1-0 win over Norwich in red shirts because of a colour clash. The Canaries took precedence as the older club.

Bath were the first to be overcome, and Wrexham were defeated in the final qualifying round after a replay at Somerton. This game remains significant a century later as the only occasion on which a County player has scored a hat-trick in the FA Cup against League opposition – Billy Devlin, the talented but injury prone little forward who had signed from Cardiff in 1919, scored all in the impressive 3-0 win. That meant a glamour tie. Newcastle away was met with enormous excitement as County prepared for their first competitive game against a top-flight side. The final game in November had seen a change in form, with County becoming draw specialists, and so dreams of giant-killing or at least bringing their illustrious opponents back for a replay were not entirely unrealistic. The record books show that County came back on the receiving end of a 6-0 hiding, but all in the 28,507 crowd – the biggest to watch County to date – felt admiration for their courage as pluck replaced luck with the side having been decimated by a particularly nasty bout of flu. Jimmy Griffin had even been stricken on the way to the game. Despite this, the first half gave Newcastle 'a fright'. Their directors visited Griffin in his hotel bed as he was too ill to return home, and they were so impressed they offered to play a friendly at Somerton, bringing in much-needed revenue and another masterful performace to th ground, as they won 5-1.

The most remarkable act of the season was down to versatile Ernie Edwards, invariably one of the star performers. The team were on the way to Millwall, and undoubtedly anxious after the previous season's welcome. If they needed to find inspiration to stir themselves for a threatening encounter while waiting for their train at Piccadilly tube station, they had to look no further than Ernie. An elderly woman slipped over the side of the platform with the sound of the train approaching. There was little time to react to this terrifying sight, but Ernie jumped down, hoisted her back up and regained his own place on the platform with seconds to spare as the train hurtled from the tunnel. His teammates could hardly let him down after such heroics, and a point was gained at the Den in a 1-1 draw.

A final memory of 1921 is a reference to the Newport County Ladies side. Little is known about them other than the fact that in one of their earliest games they beat Swansea Town Ladies 3-0. Despite it clashing with Caerleon Races, it drew a 'remarkably large crowd'. The only other report is of a game against Cardiff, also in May, and which ended in a 1-1 draw, with the kick-off being performed by rugby international George Boots.

It had been announced in March that the popular Parkes would be leaving at the end of the season. 110 applications were received and Jimmy Hindmarsh, who had caught up on his sleep to coach the reserves, was asked to step up. Fred Good also stepped down in May to be replaced as trainer by former Aston Villa star Bob Chatt, whose record of scoring the quickest ever FA Cup final goal stood until 2009 some 114 years later. At least he remains the only player to have won both the FA Cup and FA Amateur Cup. They were immediately embroiled in controversy as Plymouth fans, who had missed out on the Championship to Southampton on goal average, were livid that County had fielded a team containing five amateurs against the Saints in the penultimate game of the season. County had actually only lost 1-0, and this overlooked the fact of course that County were themselves desperate for points to avoid re-election. The colourful Cooper was released after 184 appearances, in which he certainly made himself a County legend. He was replaced by Anthony (Andy) Carr, but the disappointment of his departure was relieved by the announcement that Ernie Edwards had resigned. The press reported this with the sentiment that 'No more consistent and honest hard working player has ever served the club.' There was a stir with the (this time genuine) signing of 'Happy' Harry Hampton, the famous England international who to this day remains Aston Villa's all-time record scorer. Sadly, Harry was now forty and had been gassed in the war. He only played in sixteen games, scoring four goals, and he wasn't the only one who felt that this was a season best forgotten – unless you supported the reserves who, scored 130 goals and saw Roy McDonald become the first to be capped by Wales at amateur level. Not a single away win was recorded, and despite a new record League victory of 6-2 against Exeter, County finished rock-bottom. Chairman Johnson resigned to be replaced by Tom Crowther, but stayed to successfully plead the re-election case.

Tube hero Edwards departed at the end of the season, as did 'Ginger' Lewis who joined Cardiff, but his replacement Jimmy Carney, who was beginning a thirty-year association with the club, made one of the greatest impacts of the newcomers. The season started with a surprisingly optimistic crowd of 10,000 entertained with a 2-0 win over visitors Exeter. The season had its characteristic inconsistency, with the highlight being a 4-1 win over promotion-chasing Welsh rivals Swansea, but all in all was a huge improvement on the previous campaign, with top scorer Jack Connor being closely challenged for that honour by Tommy Lowes (both finishing on eighteen cup goals.) This new-found ability to find the net was responsible for a respectable tenth place finish. Other players also catching the eye were Jack Nicholls, who became the first Welsh cap, although he would soon to leave for Cardiff, and new signing Fred Cook, who was also destined to be a future international. The season also ended with more silverware to polish as the Monmouthshire Senior Cup made its way to Somerton.

County were beginning to resemble a professional outfit, and the discipline expected of the players was set out in the club rules. These set out the training times, arrangements for reporting injury and illness and the payment of wages. They also made it clear that players were responsible for cleaning their own kit, that friends were not allowed in the dressing room and emphasised that the instructions of the trainer must be complied with. Indeed, a training book would record any indiscretions and be reported to the board.

Sheffield Wednesday made an offer that County had no choice but to accept and Carr, who had proven a more than capable replacement for Cooper, was on his way for a club record £1,200. Jimmy (Jake) Maidment (what was it with 'keepers not using their proper names?) was brought in as his replacement and continued the fine goalkeeping standards that had been initially set by Ted Husbands. The last playing link to Ted's era, though, was severed with the departure of Groves, who had deservedly enjoyed a benefit. Sunderland-born Maidment was more interested in a different link – his uncle, Billy Charlton, was already at the club, having signed in January 1923, and was proving a

The Reserves in January 1923. Only 'keeper Billy Bray did not make a first-team appearance. Charlie Brittan (*first left, front*) and Jock Patterson (*with ball*) were selected for the Welsh League.

The reserves ended the season with silverware in the first Royal Gwent Hospital (Ince) Cup.

The earliest known action images: *Above*: Sir Garrod Thomas kicks off a practice game in front of a Somerton side, 19 August 1922. *Below*: New 'keeper Andy Carr and FA Cup action at Ninian Park v. Aberdare, 11 December 1922.

Training Rules and Players' Instructions.

1.—All players whose time is wholly engaged by the Club shall attend the Ground for training at 10.15 a.m. daily (match days excepted), and shall be under the orders of the Trainers for the rest of the day.

2.—Players engaged in business must attend training on Tuesday and Thursday evenings as early as possible, but not later than 6.30 p.m., unless excused by the Secretary.

3.—The Club Doctor is Dr. T. G. Lewis, of "Rosedale" Corporation Road, Newport, who can be seen at the above address. Any visit to the Doctor should be reported at once to the Secretary and Trainer.

4.—When a player is incapacitated by illness or injury from following his training, he must at once report the fact to the Secretary, and accompany the same with a doctor's certificate.

5.—Players must note any announcements upon the notice board in the dressing room, as they will not necessarily be advised through the post.

6.—A Training Book will be in charge of the Trainer to record any complaints which he may have to lay before the Directors when necessary.

7.—All players must clearly understand that their duties will be allotted to them by the Trainer, and the Directors inform the players his instructions MUST be carried out.

8.—It is the duty of the players to assist the Trainers in preserving cleanliness and order in the dressing rooms and upon the ground, and any player MISUSING ARTICLES used for training purposes, etc., will be liable to fines or suspension.

9.—All players are provided with outfit necessary for playing (which is the property of the Club).

10.—Match jerseys and knickers are not to be used for training purposes.

11.—Players will not be allowed to bring friends into the dressing room either during practice or on match days under any circumstances whatever, and the Trainer has strict injunctions and is held responsible for same.

12.—Players must be on the ground for home matches at least half an hour before the kick-off, and at the station for away matches at least a quarter of an hour before the departure of the train.

13.—Wages will be paid every Friday from 3 p.m. to 4 p.m. in the afternoon, and from 5 p.m. to 6 p.m. in the evening, unless otherwise notified.

14.—Any player desirous of not returning with the team from an out match, must give at least THREE DAYS' NOTICE to the Secretary in writing to get permission granted.

15.—Players are requested to note that no one is allowed in the saloon or on the brake except PLAYERS AND OFFICIALS.

16.—These Rules and instuctions are subject to any alterations the Directors may from time to time deem necessary, and due notice of any such alterations would be announced upon the players' notice board.

17.—As the Trainers are held responsible for the carrying out of these rules, they must report any breach of same.

By Order of the Directors,

Secretary.

A copy of the club rules belonging to Jack Evans.

star performer from his right-wing berth. Uncle Billy certainly helped Jake settle in, as he would miss only ten League games in the next five seasons, and also proved adept at the other end of the field by taking penalties, going on to score four goals in his 241 appearances. The Prince of Wales pub in Lincoln (he joined the 'Imps' from County) to this day has a photograph of Maidment on display. Fred and Frank McKenzie were also coming in, although the only thing they shared (apart from their surname) was the fact they were both defenders. An unusual fact is they only had nineteen toes between them, Fred being the unfortunate 'sole' with a missing digit courtesy of a blood-poisoning episode. The board were still diligently seeking to improve the ground. A roof was put on the Cromwell End terrace, and pre-season the players had proudly posed in front of the Railway End to show off their new oval, rather than square-shaped, goalposts.

By December, the previous season's top scorer and club captain Connor was also on his way to Bristol City. This time it wasn't a financially driven move, but the player himself had been disappointed with his contribution, and felt he needed fresh pastures. He incurred the wrath of supporters when flu made him miss a game – the rumour going around that he had faked illness to avoid being cup tied for any new club. His misfiring in front of goal certainly helped Billy Charlton when he was moved inside as an experiment to make his 'debut' as a centre forward at Watford – he scored four in a 5-0 win. Of course, the manager realised he had stumbled on a great latent talent, and before long he was back on the wing. That day certainly contributed greatly to his finishing as top scorer with fourteen, but none could match Fred Cook's effort against Merthyr when he mazily waltzed his way around five bewildered opponents before walking the ball into the net. Little wonder that twenty-two-year-old Cook, an ever-present face since joining, would be awarded two full Welsh caps during the season against Scotland and England.

The season itself proved to be County's best yet – it would be over a decade before they reached such dizzy heights again. In a season that would see Swansea promoted and Cardiff reach the FA Cup Final, it looked improbable that County would also go up. On 31 January, County returned from Southend with a fourth successive win in a run of twelve games with only two defeats. There were cup-winning scenes to greet the players when they arrived back at Newport station on the Fishguard mail train. Centre forward Fred Taylor, who had scored the game's only goal, was deeply embarrassed, but eventually had to accept being lofted shoulder-high and these scenes were repeated for others all the way down the High Street. Despite these celebrations, there were still sixteen games to go; perhaps the weight of expectation ultimately proved too great. A sixth-placed finish eight points behind promoted Swansea was the disappointing conclusion, with poor away form in the run in being the main reason. Six home games through the season saw the visitors steal a point, and this became the difference between success and failure. The 'handsome' Ince Cup, which was claimed to have a higher intrinsic value than the FA Cup, was returned to the boardroom when County beat New Tredegar 2-1, and a small replica with a £10 value was gifted to the club as a permanent memento.

One sad aspect of the season is the story of young Harold White, whose brother, Tom, was also at the club. He made only one first-team appearance, but was a promising inside forward for the reserves. A month later, while playing at Taunton in January 1925, he broke his knee cap after only eight minutes from a tackle by former County 'keeper Ted Lowe. He then contracted a lung disease and had to retire, dying just a few months later at the tragically young age of twenty-four.

Surely a strong foundation had been built for a serious push for promotion? Unfortunately, the next few years were extraordinarily tough, with a serious economic downturn. County, given the nature of the area, were about to feel

The team in 1925 with the replica Ince Cup.

it more than most. The club had already been forced to sell a few stars on the odd occasion, but this was about to become the norm.

Billy Charlton exited before 1925/26 began and, by the season's end, with considerable interest shown in a number of the squad, Fred McKenzie had left for Plymouth for a new club record £1,500. Cook, the talented new international star, moved to Portsmouth, where he would find glory, including a man of the match performance in the 1929 FA Cup Final. Continuing the theme suggested by these naval bases, former sailor Jack Davis had replaced Charlton and made history by becoming the first (and, through the first 100 years, the only) County player to score a hat-trick on his debut in an opening-day 4-3 win over Brighton. He repeated the feat shortly after against QPR and finished the season with a new club record of twenty goals before being promptly sold to join McKenzie at Plymouth.

There had been a change to the offside law to make it easier to score goals and perhaps this benefitted Davis, although overall only two more were scored for the season's total than in 1924/25. But it seems the defence struggled with the new rule and County, albeit never in danger of finishing in the re-election zone, had a poor seventeenth-placed finish, thanks largely to having conceded almost twice as many goals as the season before. Crowds inevitably plummeted, dropping from the 11,232 opener to half that figure within a few games, and only 3,284 for the final game against Norwich. Little wonder the fire sale had commenced. Paying the players that remained became a real challenge, reminiscent of Moss's early forays for funds, and a novel payroll system was introduced whereby married players would be paid with gate money, half crowns and florins, and the bachelor boys living in digs were paid in shillings and sixpences.

What would have been County's prospects if not forced to sell? During 1926/27, both Ted Smith and Freddie Forward joined Cook in a very successful Pompey side. The season had demonstrated the initial blind faith of County fans with a large opening day gate, and their fickleness as the numbers dropped off significantly. The lack of goals didn't help, with County ending the season as the League's lowest scorers and another future Wales international, Wilf James, capped twice at West Ham, topping the scoring charts with only nine. Wilf could even challenge Jack Cooper for eccentricity, having a habit of wearing his ever-present bowler hat even in the showers! Humiliating cup exits at the hands of minnows Poole Athletic and Lovell's hardly helped either; but this hides the real story of the season. Truth be told, County were a natural goalscorer away from challenging for promotion, and a surprising ninth-placed finish could have been so much better had there not been a devastating downturn in form, with only one win in the last eleven games costing them dearly. It didn't exactly help when Cardiff City, returning triumphant from Wembley, stopped outside Somerton to show off the FA Cup. Hindmarsh had resisted the overtures of Crystal Palace and Swansea during the season and steadfastly stuck to his task. He had to rebuild his entire forward line but, given the previous season, that was no loss. This time, new signing Archie Waterston from Musselburgh, near Edinburgh, for whom the club had splashed out the grand sum of £50, found the net with the consistency previously lacking. Although he missed twelve games in 1927/28, Waterston set a new club record of twenty-seven for the season. Frustratingly, however, the ability to score goals was at the expense of defending them, and another ninth-placed finish was the result. If only they could keep an improvement at both ends! At least the reserves won the Welsh League.

An unusual event had occurred against Luton, when the reliable Bobby

Anderson refused to take a penalty against his old club. The crowd were stunned to silence at the sight of 'keeper Maidment running the length of the field to take his first penalty as he shouted, 'It's all right, this one's going in!' Indeed, he repeated the feat in the next game. One player to have slipped in almost unnoticed was Lovell's winger, Billy Thomas. He would never be forgotten, quite possibly being County's greatest pre-war star, amassing 330 appearances in which he scored sixty-eight goals and not being dropped until 1936, when his omission nearly caused a riot. It was a worrying time, though, with gate income dropping dangerously low.

The opening day of 1928/29 was the first time that County did not include at least one new face in its opening game line up. It was an innocuous season in many ways and the club ended up bottom at Christmas. However, there was a degree of improvement in the New Year, which resulted in a sixteenth-place finish. The loyal Hindmarsh was used to having his best players sold, but he seemed to lose the plot when it came to picking his centre forward. The prolific Waterston had notched another impressive nine goals in thirteen games, but he never settled anywhere for long and moved on to Southampton in December for a healthy profit. Hindmarsh then tried almost everyone in his place, up to and including goalkeeper Len Blakemore. A penalty fell to him, and he would have sensationally justified the manager's bold experiment had the crossbar been considerably higher! Stan Bowsher had also been sold in January and was capped just two days later. He therefore went in the Welsh international record books as a Burnley player, even though he had yet to play for them. Season 1929/30 saw yet more inspired business by Hindmarsh. Caerau-born twenty-five-year-old Tudor Martin had suffered a cartilage injury and been released by West Brom. He failed to make an early impression, but came into the side in November and promptly set about breaking records that would stand the test of time and turn him into himself a true County legend. Sadly, crowds were very poor and who knows how low they may have dropped given such hard economic times had it not been for Tudor's exploits. A phenomenal thirty-four League goals in just twenty-nine League games and a season total of thirty-seven would not be broken. Nor would his club record-breaking five in one game against Merthyr in what has remained the record win at 10-0. Forty-two years later, supporter Ira Headworth recalled, 'The crowd kept begging Merthyr 'keeper Lyndon to "Let it go in Albert!" and often he obliged! Martin scored five in a row. One wag shouted, "Play the game Tudor!" to everyone's delight. Then came two superb goals by Jimmy Gittins and finally the tenth by that bow-legged

Far right: Capped Billy Thomas, one of the two best pre-war players. He made 330 appearances.

Right: Record scorer Tudor Martin visiting in 1973.

genius Billy Bagley, who later left County for Portsmouth.'

In the mid-1980s, I lived by another new signing that season, Ron Hugh, who was at right-back in that game. Ron told me, 'Andrew it was embarrassing after a while – more like shooting practice, and I honestly felt sorry for them. Not as sorry and embarrassed as I did for myself though the same season when I played for Wales against Ireland and we lost 7-0!' I can remember Ron also chuckling, saying that Merthyr may have been saved had it been raining heavily as the pitch became a swamp, making shooting impossible for most. He added, 'On more than one occasion, I can remember a penalty not going more than 12 inches at the Railway End as they couldn't scoop the ball out of the mud!' Martin had also played in the Ireland game, and it was inevitable that despite the board's promises to stop selling their stars, he would be on his way – and off he went after the penultimate game of the season, netting a hat-trick in his final appearance against Exeter before joining Wolves for £1,500, along with Cyril Pearce. Without him, County played the return at rock-bottom Merthyr in their last ever Football League game, and lost 5-1. The 1930s had arrived and depression had truly set in. Within a year, County were following Merthyr out of the League.

1930/31 – after all that hard toil, dreams are shattered as County head out of the Football League.

3

IF AT FIRST YOU DON'T
SUCCEED ...

... Then try, try again! Throughout County's story, one striking feature is the refusal to roll over and resign Newport to being represented by a lesser level of football. When the club reformed in 1989, one fanzine was the aptly named *Never Say Dai*, and it was precisely that defiance in the face of the greatest setbacks that was needed in spades at the conclusion of 1930/31, when the result of all of the hard work and heartache of the previous almost twenty years was heart wrenchingly torn away with demotion from the Football League.

The depression, coupled with supporters feeling dejected by the constant sale of stars, meant that crowds were at an all-time low. The revolving door again saw supporters learning a host of new names. Martin was followed out by Maidment, Anderson and others and their replacements, apart from makeweight Pearce, failed to make an impression. Pearce had impossible boots to fill and Martin underlined that in an April friendly with Wolves, scoring a hat-trick. However, to be fair to Cyril, he had a real go, scoring twenty-six in just thirty games. While only sixty-nine were scored in the League, four clubs netted fewer and the real problem was at the other end, with 111 conceded. That meant a bottom of the table finish. Two trips to London saw 7-1 defeats, although in a season of few highs, Bournemouth, who had been 2-0 up after just six minutes, returned home after a 7-3 trouncing. The player who demonstrated the greatest inability to defend shots was Corporation Road product Jack Clifford. Perhaps 'keeper Len Blakemore wanted him to know what it was like to be peppered all day, and accidentally filled him with pellets when out shooting wildlife. Billy Thomas was capped twice, but the sheen of that honour was dimmed a little by the fact that Wales had been unable to call on players with English clubs. One interesting snippet in a thoroughly miserable year was the appearance of Stanley Rouse at Somerton as referee for the Swindon game. Only 2,872 were there and would have had no idea that the man in the middle would one day be knighted and become the president of FIFA.

Merthyr had failed in their re-election bid, but although this was to be County's second in less than ten years, they were reasonably confident (though Aldershot were thought to have support to replace them). Any nervousness was because County had received bad press, having been taken to court through their involvement in an illegal lottery. The faith was misplaced and in fact it was Mansfield, who tallied six more votes than County, who would replace them. Chairman George Nixon immediately rallied support and proclaimed, 'The County's claims are bound to be recognised by the Football League sooner or later, for Newport is an important town which demands a club of higher standing.'

Playing once more in the Southern and Welsh Leagues, Nixon resolutely supported Hindmarsh in retaining many of his squad in an effort to force a quick return. The lottery debacle meant County were banned from the FA Cup, so could not look forward to testing their credentials even in that competition, which was a shame for supporters wondering if new top scorer Frank Peed was the real deal. Peed was yet another County player to have changed his name, and although he was another Corporation Road schoolboy product, he was actually born in Argentina as Francisco Enrique Gonzalez. Another local youngster to earn his spurs that season was George Kitson, born just 50 yards from the ground, who would remain a fixture at the club for decades.

County scored seventy in just twenty-four Southern League games, including 11-1 and 10-2 thrashings of Barry and Taunton, and on eleven occasions scored four or more as the opposition was hopelessly outclassed. Peed's total in both leagues was an astonishing forty-six in fifty-six games! Performances tailed off from March and County actually only finished sixth, perhaps having spread themselves too thinly over both leagues, also finishing second in the Welsh League. It could not have helped the players to focus when constantly reading about creditors' threats to enter County into liquidation. Bookmaker Jimmy Jones bought the ground from Lysaght's for £7,500 and shortly after 'flipped' it to Cardiff Greyhound Racing Co., who redeveloped it for their own purposes to the configuration more familiar to supporters until its demise in the 1990s, with the demolition of the banks on the Somerton Road side and Railway End, relocation of the pitch 20 yards from the Cromwell End and construction of the racing track.

A rare bit of luck came through misfortune for struggling Thame, whose crowds were so low that Luton actually framed their cheque for their share of the gate. When the Oxfordshire club resigned from the Football League, County's lobbying went into overdrive and they were voted back in. Other than Gillingham, this was to be the only occasion a club was readmitted in the days of re-election, before automatic promotion was introduced. Worries over a playing venue remained but agreements were reached with the new owners, including building the main grandstand. Supporters worked like Trojans to create the new terracing. Hindmarsh needed to rebuild his squad on a shoestring and relied on the ability of new trainer Tommy Gibbon to get the most out of them. 'General' Jimmy Gittins remained for his fourteenth and final season. He was a part-timer, also working at Braithwaite's, explaining his absence from many team photographs. By season's end he had made 309 appearances, scoring eighty-three goals.

Football is full of strange coincidences and the final-day opponents of their previous life in the League, Clapton Orient, returned for the opening fixture, but almost 6,000 extra turned out this time. They were soon brought back down to earth despite fielding a number of full and amateur internationals. It took four games for their first goal, which was scored by Bob Weale, and after eleven games the side could not boast a single victory. The season ended with another re-election plea with a warning not to expect further leniency and little to fondly recall other than a double over Cardiff, who had been relegated, with County fans enjoying *Schadenfreude* after their stop off just a few years before with the FA Cup.

If the modern-day 'Who Are You?' chant had been popular back then with the Cromwell Enders, it would have been aimed at their own side in 1933/34, as Hindmarsh heeded the warning and retained only five of the twenty-six players to wear the shirt the previous season. The newbies proved to be draw specialists and with Cardiff now facing re-election, County finished eighteenth. A canvas screen had been erected part way through the season to prevent the town's unemployed enjoying a free view and by the end of the following season, with nine of the final ten games lost, ensuring another bottom place, it was perhaps proving more beneficial in protecting their eyes. Hindmarsh had been taken seriously ill in September. Add to this the stress of yet another uphill struggle, in a season during which he and the players had

1932/33 – The boys are back – for another season of struggle!

offered to take a 25 per cent pay cut, and it is understandable why the man with an astute eye for signings with a resale value finally resigned after many years of hard work and loyal service, saying, 'I'm giving someone else the chance to change the club's luck.' Chairman Nixon again did wonders himself, gathering enough votes to be re-elected. Ex-England international Louis Page replaced him, and a full-time secretary was appointed so that for the first time the manager could concentrate on team affairs. Despite these woes, the board was increased and further terracing improvements made. As you would expect, Page made wholesale changes, with nine new faces in the opening game. Indeed, he improved the position by one whole place as County finished one up from bottom in 1935/36. Nevertheless, crowds were up, presumably enjoying seeing plenty of goals, even if their own side was on the receiving end. County were somehow again re-elected, but even Bert Moss could take no more and resigned, together with half the board.

Perhaps it was a subliminal gesture to better fortify the defence, but 1,000 tons of soil from Newport Castle was used in the summer for bank improvements, and this coincidentally saw the defence concede fewer than

100 League goals for the first time in years (ninety-eight to be precise). Early on, for the second season running, supporters were gathering after a game to, well, let's say, give advice. The first occasion had seen Moss surrounded by a police guard to answer the critics – little wonder he had resigned! That was the trigger to sign some soon-to-be-legendary names, including Lance Carr, Harry Duggan and Norman Low, who signed for a record £1,750. This led to a better placing (nineteenth) and a decent run in the Welsh Cup, going out in the semi-final 3-2 to Rhyl. Crowds had been extremely encouraging and a final positive point was the reserves winning the Welsh League.

There was a renewed belief in the club's prospects going into 1937/38. Page was putting together a team that would be celebrated for many generations. There were two Billy Owens on the books, so they were renamed 'W. M.' and 'W. E.' – the 'M' and 'E' standing for Manchester and Exeter respectively. But the squad now read like a future Hall of Fame. The expensively assembled side began with a draw and two defeats, so Page was sacked. Page had also been stricken by illness, but was as shocked as anyone and took County to court for wrongful dismissal. He won, but it was a hollow victory as the little-known Billy McCandless had already taken his place and was about to reap the dividends of Page's squad-shaping. In October, Cardiff visited for a 1-1 draw witnessed by the all time ground record of 24,268, with supporters perched precariously on the main stand roof. It took a day to count the coinage. County also played their first game in Europe, losing 6-2 in Rotterdam against a Combined Dutch XI. Another Welsh Cup semi-final appearance saw defeat, this time by Shrewsbury, and a further improved sixteenth position was secured.

Captain and full back Jimmy Kelso had been an influential figure and was looking forward to the 1938/39 campaign as much as the most fanatical of supporters. The previous season, Kelso had acted as talent spotter when half the Llanelly side failed to appear for a Welsh League game. He joked that the rest of the side be recruited from the crowd and this was agreed, with Llanelly asking him to make the selections. During the close-season break, he had a letter from McCandless, in response to his politely asking to be paid. McCandless casually ended by referring to a continued interest from Cardiff, but making it clear he did not intend to start breaking up such a promising side. Two weeks later, Kelso was sold and on his way to Ninian Park, triggering letters from fans with one complaining, 'They will be saying in a month or so that they think we have a promotion team this season and the fans will be soft enough to believe them.' In 1938/39 County were promoted as champions.

McCandless may well have been frustrated in losing Kelso but he

TELEPHONE: NEWPORT 3300   ALL CORRESPONDENCE TO BE ADDRESSED TO THE SECRETARY   TELEGRAMS: "SOCCER." NEWPORT

NEWPORT COUNTY
ASSOCIATION FOOTBALL CLUB LTD.

MEMBERS OF

FOOTBALL LEAGUE—DIVISION III. (SOUTHERN)
SOUTHERN LEAGUE,   WELSH LEAGUE (DIVISION I.)
WELSH FOOTBALL ASSOCIATION

COLOURS: RED AND WHITE JERSEYS, BLACK KNICKERS WITH RED SEAM

Directors:
COUNCILLOR A. A. WRIGHT, CHAIRMAN.
CAPT. H. J. PETTY, VICE-CHAIRMAN.
MR. G. E. NIXON.
MR. W. E. WADE.
MR. C. V. WOOD.
COUNCILLOR J. R. WARDELL.

Manager:
MR. W. McCANDLESS.

Secretary:
MAJOR H. D. CHEESEMAN.

Asst. Secretary:
MR. A. O. MENZIES.

WINNERS:
SOUTHERN LEAGUE CUP   1936-37
WELSH CHALLENGE CUP   1936-37
WELSH LEAGUE (DIV. 1.)   1936-37

Registered Office and Ground:

SOMERTON PARK,

NEWPORT,

18th June   193 8.

Mr Jas. Kelso,
Murray's Farm,
Cardross.

Dear Jas.,

Glad to hear from you, even if it is money you are after, but the Major knows that you would'nt let a weeks wages stand between your friendship for him?

I have been away a lot lately and have'nt had an opportunity of going into the matter, but will do so and forward whatever you are short.

Regarding things here, I would say that the outcome is a bit of a problem, but I hope the present Board will be able to carry on as they are a decent lot, and the harmony at the moment is excellent.

We have been doing a lot of Painting and you will be surprised at the difference when you get back.

Cardiff are still chasing after you, but I am hoping that our team will not be broken up, of course one never knows these hard times.

Regards from all at Somerton.

Yours sincerely,

Wm McCandless

Opposite: Letter from McCandless to Kelso.

Right: Supporters' letters to the *Argus* in response to Kelso's transfer.

Below: 1937 at Somerton Park, from left: Norman Low, Tommy Wood, Lance Carr, Roy John, Jimmy Kelso, Ben Williams and Harry Duggan.

used the proceeds with devastatingly good effect. Replacing him was the uncompromising Bill Roberts, while the left back berth saw the introduction of the cultured Len Richards. Behind them in goal was new 'keeper Alex Ferguson, and inside forward Arthur Hydes was another to come in and add the finishing touches to a side worthy of being called champions. Everyone was in a good mood as Neville Chamberlain assured the country that Hitler had promised him that he would not contemplate fighting Britain. Orient yet again were the opening game opponents, this time at their place, and County took the points with a 3-1 win. Brought down to earth by losing 2-1 at Port Vale, County then had a tasty home derby against Cardiff. The 18,387 crowd was a few thousand behind the record set the year before, but looks from photographs to be suspiciously low with supporters again somehow gaining access not only to the top of the stand, but also the screen obscuring the view from the bridge. They were treated to the confusing sight of County playing in all black with amber hoops. The kit for the previous few seasons had been red-and-white stripes and the news was met again with delight that they would revert to black and amber, but someone misread the order and the reverse was manufactured and had to be used until the proper strip was available.

This was the start – County won 3-0 with Hydes, who would end top scorer, getting a brace. By October, County were at the top and would not be dislodged. The Boxing Day game at Swindon was eagerly awaited and if Father Christmas had appeared with Rudolph there would have been no greater shock, as County lost 8-0. In 1973, Ira Headworth recalled the game, saying, 'Impossible – with the strongest defence in the League? They must have been tight at Christmas. Yes that was it – they were all drunk! We also made note of that outstanding player Bill Lucas, who had been the cause of all the mischief!' At 6-0 down, the formidable Roberts was heard to shout, 'Come on lads – we are still in with a chance!' The following day, County had revenge, winning a thriller 6-4. New Year's Eve then saw the double over Cardiff – 2-1 in front of almost 40,000. Promotion was secured on 15 April, 3-0 against Southend at Somerton courtesy of Albert Derrick, Arthur Hickman and Tommy Wood's 35-yard special. Players were carried aloft in delirious celebration. Of course, there had to be some stress, and this was provided by disgruntled former chairman A. A. Wright, who obtained a court judgement as a creditor owed over £4,500. The euphoria surrounding the club meant that the funds were found to pay him off. The mayor, Alderman Wardell, who had been a director from the outset, put on a celebration dinner at the Kings Head Hotel attended by Stanley Rouse, now FA secretary, and six supporters selected through a

Albert Derrick leads the assault on Cardiff as fans cling to the main stand roof ...

... and almost fall off the screen shielding Somerton Bridge as Arthur Hydes scores the second goal!

ballot. For others, there was also an event at the Little Theatre in Dock Street, of which Headworth also recalled,

> With hundreds clamouring outside for admission, the theatre was packed as the curtains parted amidst thunderous applause, revealing a stage full of strange looking men – strange that is to the audience who were used to seeing them in jerseys and knicks than everyday dress. Everyone present seemed to expect the players to break into song and dance. Lance Carr looked taller in civvies whereas little Billy (W. E.) Owen looked even smaller in everyday clobber. Norman Low of course looked immaculate and quite the matinee idol, being tall, dark and good looking. Fergie the goalkeeper was still the giant he looked on the field. The girls present screamed just as loud as they do nowadays!

NEWPORT COUNTY A.F.C. 1938-39

A. Morris, J. Webb, A. Hydes, W. Roberts, W. Hares

E. Thomas, Asst. Trainer   W. M. Owen, A. Hickman, R. Lawrence, A. Ferguson, C. Reid, N. Low, T. Mead, L. Richards, A. H. Thomas, Asst. Sec.   W. McCandless, Secretary-Manager

W. Poyntz, Trainer   Dr. W. E. Wade, A. Derrick, Mr. C. V. Wood, H. Duggan, Capt. H. J. Petty, L. Carr, Mr. J. R. Wardell, T. Wood, Mr. G. E. Nixon

R. Wilcox, R. Mogford, J. Harvey, E. Brinton, D. Williams, W. E. Owen, G. Hogg, L. Cureton, J. Sockett

The legends line up.

4

THE FIGHT IS OVER – WAR BEGINS

What should have been the most eagerly awaited season for a County fan was in fact a traumatic anticipation of another war and, having experienced its true horror, this time there was no misguided feeling that all would be over by Christmas. Welsh international Walter Robbins was the most significant of three new signings, but was not selected for the opening game at home to Southampton on 26 August, when 13,300 crammed into Somerton to see Alderman Wardell lead the team out and cheered them to an outstanding 3-1 win, thanks to another two goals from Hydes and one by Hickman. Just four days later, a reminder that County had stepped up a level came in the form of a visit by Spurs, and another Hickman effort shared the spoils in a 1-1 draw. The crowd was now 19,500 and a sign of just how far County had come, with the days of re-election looking a distant memory. The only way was up – or it should have been! That very day, the government called up the armed forces reservists with a half-time announcement asking for all Monmouthshire Territorial Volunteers to report to their depots. Ira Headworth reminisced,

The atmosphere was suddenly rent by the crackling loudspeakers asking us to listen to an important announcement by the mayor. The well known voice of Alderman Jack Wardell, with his familiar Wolverhampton twang, warned us with regret that this might be our last match prior to what looked certain to be war – and of course war there duly was. What a gloomy way to start a match! We tried to put out of our minds what the mayor had said but we all knew he was right and the match was to be a memorable one following which history was to prove right those 'Dismal Jimmies' who had pessimistically predicted that should County ever win promotion there would be a war! The following Saturday we lost 2-1 at Nottingham Forest and this truly was our last match before the storm, for war was declared the following day. The excellent opening of three points in three matches was a fine start surely. What a tragedy for County was World War II.

County had in fact been forty minutes late arriving at Forest because of a rail delay, but how futile it all must have seemed with Hitler having invaded Poland that morning. September saw crowds drop dramatically for five friendlies, the first a 2-0 defeat at Cardiff in which supporters had their first glimpse of young Ray Wilcox, who would become one of the club's greatest legends. In October, football was reorganised to regional leagues, County playing in the South West. The first game was lost at home 2-0 to Swindon in front of just over 1,800. In early December, Somerton, which was already being used for the war effort, became unavailable. A blackout had been imposed and the owners took priority for its use on Saturday afternoons. County took up an offer to relocate to Rodney Parade and the first game there saw a 1-0 defeat to Bristol Rovers. In March, only 800 saw the 5-0 annihilation of Cardiff in the Welsh Cup. The season had to be extended, but the rugby club had completed their fixtures and the Rodney Parade ground was needed for cricket, so County moved into the cramped Rexville home of Lovell's Athletic for the final five games, all of which were won by large scores, including 11-0 against Torquay – but this time only 500 were there to see it, 100 fewer than the previous game when Cardiff were again embarrassed 4-1. It had already been agreed to disband before the last game when Plymouth suffered 5-2. In fact, the previous day, the same fixture was played there (this time won 6-3) and County had agreed pay toward their overnight expenses. That led to a further game months later on Christmas Day against Lovell's in order to meet that debt. The match programme carried an assurance that County would be back after the war, with the comment that could easily be used to sum up the club's existence all these years later: 'Newport County has thrived on its difficulties, and it still lives.'

In April 1945, with the war over in Europe, a new board was formed taking on over £15,000 in liabilities. On 1 July, McCandless was reappointed and made clear the club's position: 'We are not starting at rock-bottom but 100 yards below!' The ground was a disaster zone and the players' appearances

Alderman Wardell proudly led the team out against Southampton and no doubt cheered as the Saints defence retrieved the ball from the net after Hyde's opening goal.

Many players joined Lovell's and enjoyed outstanding success during the next five years – seen here in 1943/44 including Ferguson, Low, W. M. Owen and future stars Bill Lucas and Doug Witcomb.

after years of hardship may have shocked supporters not tempted to follow Lovell's exploits. County would inevitably have to comprise a mix of veterans and youngsters.

Ray Wilcox had seen his development halted in terms of League games, although he joined the RAF touring India with Tommy Walker's all stars team. He remembered McCandless many years later, saying, 'He was an old fashioned type of manager. The first team only saw him when he announced the side and when he sat on the line during the match.'

Regional leagues were set up for 1945/46, with teams allowed to field up to six guests. The fixture list was certainly attractive with the likes of Arsenal, Chelsea, Aston Villa, West Ham and Wolves providing the stiffest of opponents. Little wonder there were some heavy defeats, not helped by failing to field a settled side, with no fewer than forty-eight players making an appearance. The first game was a 2-1 defeat at Brentford with Derrick scoring, and fans must have felt very mixed emotions when no fewer than eight of the promotion side were humbled 5-1 by Fulham when Somerton opened its doors once more. The FA Cup was played over two legs, County going out in the third round after losing 4-3 at the Dell in front of 22,000 and the return 2-1. The first round had been notable as the kit was stolen; it would eventually be found scattered along Chepstow Road.

Confidence was not exactly at its best as County got ready to resume life properly in the Second Division in 1946/47. McCandless left bitterly on 9 April, after falling out with the board about the club's future direction and became Cardiff manager in June, going on to lead all three south Wales clubs to promotion. His replacement in May was the celebrated England star Tom Bromilow, whose Crystal Palace side had pushed County close for the championship. He was another from the school that believed that player preparations should be left to the trainer, so he brought in Jimmy Marshall to fulfil that role. Marshall had another unusual responsibility on London rail platforms, as explained to me one day by Andy McBlain who signed in the February:

Ladies of the night would try and tempt us players with offers of '£5 for short time'. Marshall would be going frantic trying to keep them away from us. There really was no need though as that would have seen off half our wage! On Mondays, he would make us all walk to a golf course and play a few rounds. Some of us didn't like golf and Marshall would watch us like a hawk or we would sneak off under the cover of the trees to play cards!

One of County's most successful managers, Billy McCandless.

Of Bromilow he added, 'I can't ever recall him even giving a team talk!'

The first game was a heavy 6-1 defeat at Nottingham Forest – coincidentally their last League opponents – with the only goal scored by Fred Leamon. That was followed by a 3-2 defeat at Burnley before Coventry became the first visitors to Somerton. County won 4-2 in front of 14,104 but it proved a false dawn. Fundraising went into overdrive to invest heavily in strengthening the side, but new bodies were not available in time for the calamitous trip to Newcastle on 5 October. What remains a record crowd for a County game of 52,137 were eagerly looking forward to seeing their own new 'Magpie', debutant Len Shackleton, later dubbed the 'Clown Prince of Soccer'. A missed penalty by Newcastle meant that they could only equal what remains the record score in a League game; with Shackleton scoring six, they romped home 13-0. County's unfortunate 'keeper that day was Charlie Turner, who one day told me, 'Shackleton could make the ball sing and had decided that day to show his new club's fans exactly what he could do. We were just there to make up the numbers! The only bit of luck I had was not getting dropped after the Newcastle game because the reserve 'keeper let in 11 that day as well!' Sam Prangley was Turner's close friend and teammate, and grateful not to have played that day. Sam went to meet the team arriving back shamefaced at the station and also told me,

> We would always joke with him about that Newcastle game – they had such a pasting! He would say, 'It was ok for you lot out there – what about me!' And then he would say, 'I didn't mind their players, it was the buggers behind the goal I didn't like – especially the policeman who kept laughing every time I let one in!'

Charlie at least enjoyed a much better time, despite losing 3-0 against Manchester City. At the end of the game, the legendary England 'keeper Frank Swift, who died in the Munich Air Disaster, ran the length of the pitch to shake his hand in admiration of a defiant performance. Yet another 'Corpa Road Boy', Prangley had been one of many signings during the season, but in his case a reluctant one from Lovell's: 'They were only Southern League, but were much better organised than County. I wouldn't say that my first impressions of County, therefore, were good! It was raggedy-tag training and your kit would be there today, but tomorrow you wouldn't know where it was!' Another signing was tough playboy striker Frank Rawcliffe. McBlain told me, 'Frank played hard on and off the field and I was very strongly advised not to go out drinking with him!' Prangley added,

SIX-GOALS SHACKLETON "ROBBED"

'Six-goals Shackleton Robbed'.

This is one time Shackleton did not score. Oldham, the Newport left back, is seen taking the ball from the £13,000 forward's toes.

He was a devil of a boy! He would always be in the pub on the corner at the back of the station. He wasn't at training the one day and Jimmy Marshall told George Kitson 'Go fetch him.' When he eventually got there he said to Marshall, 'Listen Jimmy, I know you – you used to play with my father and he told me all about you!' He was a big strong fella and a real handful, but would be as friendly as anything with anyone in the pub!

Bromilow bemoaned a long injury list, blaming it on weakness caused through the war years, but his plea for extra rations was rejected. He even contemplated at one time sending players to Ireland where rationing was not in force! He could not, however, blame the board for lack of support. An impressive £9,000 was spent on signings, including Eddie Carr, who would become one of the club's most popular ever players; Harold Williams, who would become the first full international since Billy Thomas; and long-serving Doug Hayward, who told me he had a different reason than Turner for remembering the Manchester City game: 'I got hit in the privates during the game and could do no more that day!'

A dreadful winter and flooding meant the season was extended until June. In May, Burnley visited for the first all-ticket game at Somerton. Only 14,751 of a much larger crowd were actually recorded, as many more broke the gates open and forced their way in. The final game saw sweet revenge against Newcastle, winning 4-2 and costing the visitors their promotion! However, the

League table doesn't lie, and County finished bottom with 133 goals conceded.

Season 1947/48 started well but was unspectacular with a twelfth-place finish, although the bank manager at least was pleased with the gate receipts from an average crowd of 11,443.

The 1948/49 campaign began as per usual with numerous new signings, although the team sheet would start to have a familiar look for the next few years to come. Ray Lawrence had also returned as trainer, but he had his work cut out and it took eleven games to chalk the first win. Reg Parker had signed in the summer from Cardiff, scoring on his debut against Bournemouth on the opening day, and he must have felt mightily frustrated as he scored six before enjoying a win bonus. Parker was to finish as joint top scorer with Carr, both on twenty-three. More impressively, he would finish his County career in 1954 with 110 goals in 226 appearances. This included ninety-nine League goals and he suffered typical County misfortune by being deprived of the 100 mark by an abandoned game. Nevertheless, Reg has remained the top scorer through the entire history of the club, and at the time of writing looks in no danger of being overtaken.

Eddie Carr – fifty-five goals in 109 appearances.

NEWCASTLE UNITED

ASSOCIATION FOOTBALL CLUB

ST. JAMES'S PARK, NEWCASTLE UPON TYNE

OFFICIAL PROGRAMME - 2d.   No. 8.

NEWCASTLE UNITED

FOOTBALL LEAGUE FIXTURE

VERSUS

NEWPORT Co.

KICK-OFF **3-15** P.M.

SATURDAY, OCT. 5th, 1946.

'Nightmare at Newcastle' match programme.

Crindau School product and County's all-time record goalscorer, Reg Parker.

Doug Hayward made his debut in 1946 and made 242 appearances over the next ten years.

5

CHIMES, GUNNERS AND COCKERELS – IN THE CUP

The 1948/49 season may well have been forgettable in the League, but the FA Cup was to be an altogether different matter. Against all odds, County enjoyed what still remains their best ever cup run – all the way to the fifth round. In fact, for the next decade it really was really more about the romance of the cup than ever threatening to repeat the exploits of 1938/39, although the nation and indeed the rest of the world were no doubt grateful for a respite from war.

County's 1948/49 FA Cup run was expected to be short lived, coming on the back of a run of poor form, but three new additions were to make a huge impact – diminutive inside forward Len Comley, full back Lou Bradford and 'keeper Alec Grant. The first round was at home to Brighton. Grant had been signed just two days before and could not play but Comley, who had already made an instant impression in his early appearances, scored twice. That saw a tricky away tie at non-league Leytonstone and County had a real fright before going through 4-3 after extra time. Next up in the third round was a far more glamorous fixture at Second Division Leeds. The cup run and new signings seemed to lift the side and the previous four games were all won, but thoughts of success at Elland Road were for dreamers – then again, that is what the FA Cup is all about! That is precisely what the rest of the country was saying when hearing that day's results, as County pulled off a shock 3-1 win through goals by George Roffi, Eddie Carr and Bobby Harper.

Confidence soared until a week later, when the legendary Tommy Lawton scored four of Notts County's goals in an 11-1 win. How were County supposed to recover from that for the fourth-round visit of First Division

Huddersfield? 22,500 fans were keen to find out and they could hardly believe their eyes. In fact, they could barely see at all in a game that ought not to have been played due to dense fog. Twice County fell behind but bravely battled back and after extra time, in which Huddersfield were desperately hanging on, the score finished 3-3. They already knew before the replay that the winners would travel to Fratton Park to meet a Portsmouth outfit that were not only unbeaten at home in over a year but were sitting proudly at the top of the First Division. Going to another First Division ground was a formidable obstacle and was in itself as glamorous and as profitable an occasion as County could have dared dreamed possible. 2,000 County fans made the long trek north and more made themselves heard in the 34,183 crowd. Under early pressure, Grant in particular performed heroics, but midway through the first half County scored not once but twice through Carr and Parker. Huddersfield

Ray Wilcox (*right*) prepares for the kick-off at Somerton against Huddersfield with their legendary Irish International captain Peter Doherty.

quickly responded, but in the second half Parker again netted to make it 3-1 and County never looked in danger. They say on a still night you can still hear the strains of 'Mae Hen Wlad Fy Nhadau' as County's delirious fans chaired the giant-killers off the pitch. There were even greater scenes of hysteria awaiting the team at Newport station, with over 5,000 gathering and making it impossible for the mayor to give his official civic greeting. Danny Newall was carried aloft over the Newport Bridge toward Corporation Road, despite his desperate pleas that he had moved house.

That set things up perfectly for the visit to Portsmouth and 8,000 travelling fans did their best to silence the famous Pompey Chimes, whose numbers had been swelled to a new ground record of 48,851. Pompey were top of the First Division in a season in which they would finish champions, five points clear of Manchester United. In contrast, County were third from bottom of the Third Division (South). After just three minutes, a rare slip by Ray Wilcox let in Len Phillips and it looked as though the floodgates would open. Almost 50,000 people and many more around the country could scarcely believe it when half-time arrived with County 2-1 up. Harper and Carr had truly muffled those famous Chimes and it was a choir of Welsh voices that greeted the players for the second half. After twelve minutes Phillips scored again, but with fifteen minutes remaining County could have pulled off not just the shock of the day but one of the greatest giant-killings of all time. Parker's header hit the bar and fell to Carr, who had the easiest of tasks to slot it home, despite the presence of not only the 'keeper but full back Ferrier stood on the line. It was a certain goal and would have been, had the referee not forgotten the laws of the game and given offside. In extra time, Comley missed an open goal. Wilcox stopped a goal-bound shot with his hands, but Grant made a breathtaking save from Barker's penalty. County looked well worth the lucrative replay. Then, with just five minutes remaining, Scottish international and future County manager Jimmy Scoular created the opportunity for the England star Jack Froggatt to score the decisive winner. The match ended 3-2 and County were out (but not down) as they returned home as the pride of Wales.

Some of the stars of that legendary side in later years shared their memories of the Cup run with me.

Doug Hayward:

The Cup game at Leeds was probably the best we played in my time there. We could do nothing wrong that day. I was playing against an Irish international and never gave him a kick. We were so very unlucky in the fifth round at

Alec Grant clears from the dangerous Pompey forwards, while in the following two photographs, Reg Parker shows he is every bit as much a threat to First Division defences.

County go wild as Harper makes it 1-1.

The team that almost silenced the 'Pompey Chimes'. *Back (from left)*: Newall, Hayward, Roffi, Grant, Bradford, Parker, Morrall. *Front (from left)*: Harper, Carr, Wilcox, Comley, Williams.

Portsmouth. They were the top team in the country and we must have taken 10,000 supporters. There were nearly 50,000 there! They scored first but we got two before they got another one and took it into extra time. Alec Grant was a good 'keeper for us and he saved a penalty, but they managed to get another one just before the end. We were really disappointed as we thought we had them for a replay and I believe we could have got to the semi-final as we would have played Derby next, who I think we would have beaten as they were nothing special.

Len Comley:

I got two against Brighton, but it was my assist for Reg Parker that sticks in my mind. As the ball came to me I shouted 'Reg' and let it go straight through my legs to him. Lovely little dummy it was! Would you believe it though, the toughest game we had was in the next round at Leytonstone, a London amateur club. They had two great players – one was a bald headed amateur International. We went one down – then two – then three – oh dear oh dear! We goes in at half-time and fair-do's, Bromilow didn't lose his temper, he just said, 'You can do better.' We did – we won 4-3! Raich Carter was the Leeds manager and I scored. There were over 30,000 there for that game. As we were coming off the pitch at the end, Tom Bromilow was on the side shaking our hands and Carter was alongside him looking furious! Apparently their players had all been promised a suit by a local tailor if they had beaten us! Roland Depear and Harrison Fearnley played for them and joined us later. Depear was huge – he must have been about six foot six! Of course my good mate Harold Williams went the other way and joined them.

County had survived the biggest panic before the Huddersfield game – goalkeeper Alec Grant had gone missing! Having travelled up the night before, Grant's bed had clearly not been slept in. Where was he? There was much relief and amusement when it was discovered that he had slept all night in the wrong hotel room! Len told me:

I can remember that, Andrew, now you mention it. He was another nice chap and a good goalkeeper. He was a bit different though and used to read books at half-time like Dickens and George Bernard Shaw! We went to a show the night before in Huddersfield and me and Harold went backstage and had our photo taken with two of the girls – Dutch I think they were. I got in trouble with the

Len Comley.

wife over that one! What I best remember about the game is that it had been snowing and it was so bloody cold. We got to the ground early and I went to the toilet and could hear this noise coming from the baths – they had two of them. It was perishing and there was Alec in a freezing bath! He said to me and Harold, 'Come on in – it will do you good.' We ran like hell! I used to travel to Newport with Harold as I stayed living in Swansea. We couldn't get on our train to go back home and most of us players were smuggled out of the station through a back entrance. Me and Harold would train at the Vetch and go up to Newport on a Thursday, getting the bus to Cardiff and then the train. One day the bus caught fire the other side of Bridgend. They were all panicking but me and Harold just stood around the back by the exhaust. All of a sudden a load of smoke belched out and covered us – we were black! We had to go on to Newport like that. In the papers it said that we had been heroes and saved everyone!

Len summed up Pompey quite simply:

We should have beaten them. I was no more than four paces away from Froggatt when he got their winner – I was so close to stopping him – if only! The Supporters' Club were going to buy a commemorative watch for each of us, with our names on the back and details of the match, but the FA stopped it – why, I don't know!

Harold Williams:

After I'd played against Leeds they couldn't get me there quick enough! Jimmy Milburn was marking me and he wasn't quick enough for me. Alec Grant was a character! He was a schoolteacher and always had his head in a book, but we didn't rib him over that as he was a good 'keeper and he had the respect of the team. Those games showed what we were capable of and even though we were not doing well in the League we took that confidence into the game at Portsmouth. The noise when we came out was tremendous – there was thousands from Newport and they were having a great day out. They scored very early after Ray Wilcox slipped. What an absolute gentleman he was – a truly lovely guy – very unassuming and he was always a good player and was one of the best in my time there; although George Roffi could have gone on to be an outstanding player. Danny Newall was also a good player – although I don't think there was many better than me! Bobby Harper, who was little like me and played on the opposite wing, scored and we really had our heads up then. Jimmy Scoular was playing for them and he would have kicked his granny that one; but we took them into extra time and although we lost 3-2 I still think we should have won. That was my most memorable game at Newport aside from playing for Wales.

Williams indeed was capped twice that season and although a £12,000 offer was turned down from Sheffield United after the Leeds game, he was on his way at the end of the season to form a lethal partnership at Leeds with his lifelong best friend, the great John Charles, with Roland Depear coming in part exchange. The Leeds 'keeper Harrison Fearnley would also find himself at Somerton the following season.

Season 1949/50 also saw Grant leave as he could not find a teaching post. Injuries and illness saw County struggling by September. Welsh International Fred Stansfield signed and made an immediate impact. Irving 'Joe' Payne became the record signing at £5,000 but only made sixteen appearances and left at the end of the season having not replaced Carr, whose departure

Above: Len Comley and Alec Grant.

Right: Harrison Fearnley left Leeds and joined County.

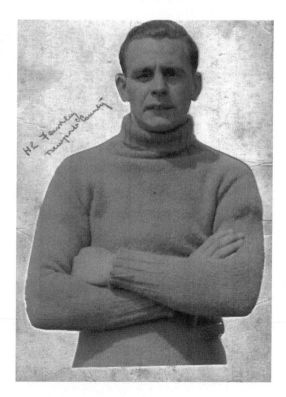

upset supporters in October. Tommy Lawton came back with defenders still trembling over the previous season's drubbing. The opportunity of seeing the England star attracted a post-war record 21,543 with fans locked out, but the unlikely hero was new signing Depear. The former Royal Marine did not exactly earn the respect of his teammates. Harrison Fearnley chuckled when he told me in his broad Yorkshire accent, 'Roland were useless', and the dignified Doug Hayward confirmed: 'He really was not very good at all!' **However,** they say everyone has one great game in them, and this was Depear's. He stopped Lawton in every conceivable way, sometimes aided and abetted by the referee! Hayward added, 'At one point, Lawton turned to me and said, "Where is that bloody centre-half from?"' However, he managed it, although it cost Lawton his place in the England side two days later against Wales. County drew 1-1.

There had been some high-scoring home wins, but losing to Port Vale in the third round of the Cup started a downward spiral. Bromilow resigned in January, with trainer Lawrence stepping up until Stansfield took over as player-manager in March. Just before then, the return to Notts County had seen another embarrassing reverse, although the circumstances were more to blame. Hayward told me,

Lawton (*right*) looks on as Depear (*left*) once more wins the race. Ray Amphlett is centre.

There was nothing in it until Harrison got injured. George Roffi was always going in goal in training so I said, 'You go in.' 'No way!' he said. I'd never played in goal in my life but gave it a go. We lost 7-0! I had another go in goal as well against Nottingham Forest (a 4-1 victory) but it was late in the game so I was ok.

Stansfield did his best, but County faced another re-election, although as the League was being extended by four clubs they were never in any danger of again losing League status.

1950/51 was a season of some wildly inconsistent results, but County finished a respectable eleventh and enjoyed another good FA Cup run to the fourth round, losing at home to top of the table Norwich, back then managed by 1938/39 hero Norman Low. Norwich's return to Somerton for the League encounter was far more memorable! Future County star Tom Docherty was in the Canaries side that day and told me,

The game was on a Good Friday and it was pouring down. The ball would just plop and stick in the mud. The game should never have been played! Norman wanted the game called off at half-time with us 2-1 down and the referee said he would if we equalised! Our 6' 6" reserve 'keeper was making his first appearance of the season and although he was brilliant in the air, Cliff Birch who had played for us and joined County that season knew of his weakness on the ground and told County to exploit it. Far from us equalising, County scored another three!

It was at this point that referee Blythe intervened and put his name into Somerton history by calling the game off in the 73rd minute with County 5-1 up! Tom continued,

It was ridiculous! The balls in those days would get extremely heavy if they were soaked and our centre half Foulkes knocked himself out heading it – by then it was like a lead weight! The crowd went wild and we couldn't get out of the car park with a couple of thousand fans after the referee's blood.

Blythe left disguised as an ambulanceman and was never seen at Somerton again, while Norwich's Wickstead at least lightened the mood by emerging disguised with an oversized fake moustache! Salt was rubbed into the wound with the rearranged game drawn 1-1, and the day after, a tired County team played a Welsh Cup semi-final replay against Merthyr. This fifth game in eight days proved too much as the Martyrs triumphed 4-1. The season ended with a Battle of Britain game at Somerton, where County beat PSV Eindhoven 3-0. While a time for celebration, the season had also seen one of the most tragic County events with the brilliant talent and hugely popular George Roffi, who had scored four in the 7-0 win against Aldershot in September, suffering a serious mental breakdown from which he never recovered. He spent the next twenty years of his life in hospital before dying there in 1973.

There was steady improvement under Stansfield in 1951/52, and had home form in any way matched the points return from away trips, promotion may have been a possibility; but it was nevertheless a satisfying sixth-place finish. In 1952/53, during which Bert Moss died, supporters enjoyed another good run to the third round of the cup, but defeat at home to Sheffield United saw a drop in form. Jackie Wharton and Les Graham were signed. Graham's eight goals avoided a dreaded re-election and secured fifteenth place. The most memorable game was at home to Coventry. Losing 4-2, any hopes of a comeback had surely vanished when full back Len Staples' ankle injury made him a limping passenger put on the left wing for nuisance value only. Len had other ideas! First he hit a 35-yard screamer to reduce the deficit and 2 minutes later, from exactly the same position, showed it was no fluke. The game finished 4-4 and ironically those were the only two goals Staples scored in his eight years at the club. The reserves won the Welsh League again.

After five games in 1953/54, County were in the unusual position of being the Division's highest scorers (and having the worst defence) despite having signed Welsh International 'keeper Iorrie Hughes to replace Harrison Fearnley, who explained his reluctant departure to me:

I were making a bit of extra money wi't my own window cleaning business. A few of t'other players would give me a hand too. The chairman, Harold John, found out and when it came to renewing my contract he said that because I had another job he would only pay me as a part timer, even though I only did my business in my spare time! I told him that I were a professional footballer and left the club, but I were very sad 'bout it.

John and his directors were actually upsetting a lot of people, and in September an extraordinary meeting of the Supporters' Club was held, following which all seven board members resigned. A shareholders' meeting in October, with over 400 present, was acrimonious, but the outcome was the establishment of a caretaker board and some money-generating initiatives. Stansfield's friend and Welsh cap Ken Hollyman was signed, but it was all too

Beriah Moore turns to his teammates after scoring in the 1951 Welsh Cup semi-final at Ninian Park, but Merthyr equalised a minute later and won the replay against an exhausted County 4-1.

Jackie Wharton and Les Graham using the state-of-the-art training facilities.

much for the manager and he resigned. Bill Lucas was playing for Swansea but trained with County while managing his pub. He returned from a game at Doncaster to find a pub full of directors, who promptly offered him the job. That started not only the recovery of that season, as form instantly improved, but an association with the club for whom his father had played in that first season that would mean the name Lucas (or, more commonly, 'Lukey') would be one of the most revered in the club's history.

Hopes of yet another FA Cup run were dashed when non-league Cambridge United knocked County out after a replay. Cup revenue was pretty much relied on by now, but in January the board dug deep and signed the main thorn in their side from that defeat – striker Len Saward. This uniquely saw County pay fees to both Cambridge and Crystal Palace, who had also retained his registration. Unfortunately, after a bright start and a starring role when Norwich were beaten 4-1, Saward was injured and things turned sour. He told me,

When I recovered, I played at Mountain Ash, in the middle of nowhere. There were about twenty people there and they had to drive sheep off the pitch so we could play! I felt really down about it. To further add to my despondency they put me in lodgings with a woman, a kindly old soul, who told me over my

Bill Lucas (*seated*) profits from beer sales with supporters shortly after joining.

porridge on my first morning that her husband had died in my bed the week before! I was out of there sharp and they put me up in the Cross Hands, but I decided that I wanted out. I was very happy indeed at Newport up until I had that injury. That six weeks out, the game in Mountain Ash and that woman's bed put the mockers on it!

The Welsh Cup also ended in frustration as County lost a semi-final replay to Chester, having beaten Swansea 6-2 in an earlier round. With another fifteenth-place finish and nothing to play for, the final game of the season was home to Ipswich, who won the championship on goal average thanks to their 2-1 victory. There is a shameful story behind that – one I have chosen not to tell.

The following season, 1954/55, was frustrating with a nineteenth-place finish. Parker retired, but in October, Tommy Johnston signed from Norwich, becoming one of County's best ever strikers, scoring fifty-three in only sixty-eight appearances. That tally did not include six in the end of season testimonial for Ray Wilcox against an International All Stars XI, who included one of football's all-time greats, Stanley Matthews. Over 500 autograph hunters invaded the pitch ten minutes from time, having to be chased off by the police; once they were settled impatiently back on the side

Saward scores in a 6-2 Welsh Cup win against Swansea in 1953/54.

they saw Tommy score his final three in an incredible four minutes as the game finished 8-8. How little did they know as they brandished pens and paper that the County 'keeper making his debut that day would become the club's all-time record appearance holder and rarely disputed No. 1 over the next fifteen years – Len Weare.

Weare told me,

Stan came into our dressing room before the game and said to 'Polly' [John Rowland], who was going to be marking him, 'Don't you kick me!' He only 'played' the first half but turned it on ... then he'd had enough! I let in eight! To be honest we wanted them to turn it on for the crowd. Our players would back off to let them have shots so I didn't get any stick for letting so many in.

Len Weare at QPR, showing the brave form that made him a County legend and member of the Newport County AFC Hall of Fame. By choice a part-time pro, he amassed 607 competitive appearances before retiring in May 1970. A reserve for the 1958 Wales World Cup squad, his loyalty to unfashionable County undoubtedly cost him the opportunity to win Welsh caps.

We were losing 8-7 with a couple of minutes to go and the ref gave us a penalty so we could draw.

The reserves once again won the Welsh League, but as their player coach Sam Prangley told me, they hardly celebrated in style. 'When we won the league, the chairman said, "Have a party." It was at Polly Rowland's father's chip shop on the top of Cromwell Road! We weren't impressed!'

Johnston remained prolific in 1955/56, hardly helped by his teammates. After an 8-1 Cup defeat to Brighton, crowds deserted in droves and form similarly nosedived. In February, Johnston was sold to Orient out of necessity, where he became such a hero in two spells that when he died in 2008 their South Stand was immediately renamed in his honour. Fortunately, re-election was averted and a nineteenth-placed finish again was secured, thanks to the return of Lucas Easter, who had been sidelined since September. So near but so far was again the story of the Welsh Cup, losing 5-2 to Swansea in the semi-final. Keith Tennant told me,

That was no shame when you look at the forward line they had: Cliffie Jones and Terry Medwin on the wings, Ivor Allchurch, Des Palmer and Harry Griffiths. I was marking Allchurch and didn't see him all day – if I had I would have kicked him! I couldn't get near him! What a forward line!

Season 1956/57 proved far more interesting. 11,371 was a markedly improved crowd buoyed by the prospect of shock signing from Cardiff, the current Welsh international full back Alf Sherwood, who was acclaimed by Sir Stanley Matthews as his most difficult opponent. Local products Harry Harris and Colin Hudson had matured impressively, Harris having scored nineteen the previous season, and new signing Pat Terry added an aggressive aerial threat. County enjoyed their best start in years with only four defeats by the end of the year, one of which was their first floodlit game at Crystal Palace. Crowds remained around the 12,000 average and Sherwood attracted admiration from teammates and fans alike. That was even more the case when he became the first County player to captain his country. This was against Scotland, and County chests puffed out when he led Wales out against England at Wembley. If Alf had rubbed off on County, perhaps some of County's notorious ill luck passed to him! Arsenal 'keeper Jack Kelsey was injured after just thirteen minutes and Alf was forced to take his place in goal. He did well enough defying the like of Matthews to keep the score to 3-1 but could not deny Tom

Sherwood goes in goal for Wales at Wembley, but how can he stop legendary Tom Finney?

Finney, though it was to be his last appearance in the red shirt.

Although playing in the Third Division, the reality was that Sherwood's successor was an inadequate replacement and already many were bemoaning the absence from squads of both Len Weare and Ray Wilcox. It is maintained to this day that both would have won many caps had they moved to bigger clubs.

Come the New Year, County were once more in the third round of the FA Cup. Their opponents at Somerton were top of the table Southampton. County had been breathing down their necks in second place, but the run up to the game was frustrating as County had suffered postponements over the Christmas period; others took full advantage and County dropped to fifth. After that, County would always be playing catch up, especially if they could vanquish the 'Saints'. The dreadful conditions did not worry the amber element of the 18,562 crowd one bit as Harris and Hudson raced County into a 2-0 lead after just eleven minutes. By fifty-two minutes, the tables had turned and County were 3-2 down until Harris looped in a late equaliser. By this time, the players were so mud-splattered that it was barely possible to distinguish one team from the other. Before the replay, the fourth-round draw was made, and the winners would play home to the 'Mighty Gunners' Arsenal, currently third in the First Division. A reshuffle was necessary at the Dell. Tom Docherty told me:

Billy Lucas took me aside on the Monday and told me to keep it to myself, but that he would be pushing me up into the forward line in place of Gordon Brown. I felt awkward about this as Gordon was one of my closest friends at the club and I used to travel to the ground with him. At the hotel before the game, Ray Lawrence announced the team; including George Thomas in my position at wing-half. Gordon was quietly sympathising with me assuming that I had been dropped and I felt awful knowing that in fact I was taking his place! Alf Sherwood got injured early on in the game and as it was before substitutes were allowed, he swapped places with me up front just for nuisance value.

Tom made light of losing Sherwood's influence at left back, tackling like a demon and using his pinpoint passing to help lay the foundation for a single goal victory courtesy of Harris. Tom added: 'Fair play to Gordon – he came straight up to me after the game and said "Tom, I could not have dropped back to full back and done that."' Harris was carried off the pitch and the scenes at Newport station were reminiscent of 1949. Weare told me, 'This is the game that most sticks out in my mind. I'm very placid, but when Harry scored I ran up and dragged him to the ground and kissed him, something we didn't do in those days!'

Around 22,500 fans crammed in for the Arsenal game would vouch that the 2-0 defeat was not a fair reflection of the game. Arsenal's Welsh international and future County player Derek Tapscott scored after just five minutes and their second came just two minutes from time. In between these two goals, County fought gallantly, prompted by man of the match Lucas, and had many opportunities to create another shock. Weare also talked to me about that game, blaming the conditions: 'The pitch was unplayable. There was 100 ton of sand on it and it was like playing on a beach. For their second I couldn't get my footing because of the pitch and so could only parry the ball to one of

Left: Chairman Percy Jones won't let go of hero Harry Harris.

Below: Future County player and Wales international Derek Tapscott puts Weare under pressure in the FA Cup.

their players and he tapped it in.' The rest of the season was an anticlimax as form fell away, and while twelfth was an improvement, there was a sense of what may have been. Southampton also lost out to Ipswich, managed by a certain Alf Ramsey. The Welsh Cup? Need you ask? County lost a semi-final replay to Swansea.

1957/58 took on great significance as it was decided to scrap the two regions for the Third Division and create a new Third and Fourth. To survive you had to finish in the top half. Colin Hudson went to Cardiff with John McSeveney, Cec Dixon and Neil O'Halloran coming the other way.

McSeveney told me about his introduction to Newport:

My brother was a pro at Motherwell and he came down for my first training session. We were doing a routine where we had to work our way past Billy Lucas. Bill was jockeying me so I chipped the ball over his head to run past him. Next thing I knew, I was lying prostrate, having been clothes-lined by Billy, who looked down at me and said, 'Don't take the p***!' My brother looked down at me and said, 'So much for you being their new star player!'

McSeveney, like all who worked with Lucas, had a host of stories to tell me. He added,

We had an old iron boiler in the middle of the dressing room, which would get red hot. Billy forgot himself this day when he was giving us a half-time rollocking and sat on it, burning his backside quite badly. We were still laughing 10 minutes into the second half! Billy also perfected a little routine, which meant that at a throw-in I would have to elbow the defender out of the way to create a bit of space before making my run. I would have to do this just as the ball reached a certain point above Billy's head. The first time we did this in a match I elbowed my man just as he had told me, but for some reason Billy halted his throw, paused and went through the routine again. Well this guy had cottoned on by now and gave me an almighty elbow to the cheek, knocking me flat out. Billy was doubled over laughing!

However, John was not so fond of another teammate, who thought himself a bit 'big time'. He added,

He was a greedy beggar and one day shot from an impossible angle when he all he had to do was square it to me for a tap in with an open goal. I gave him a mouthful and as I was walking back he jumped on me from behind and belted me! I thought,

Tapscott scores Arsenal's first goal in 2-0 defeat of brave County.

New recruits McSeveney, O'Halloran and Dixon off to a flying start on 27 July 1957.

'That's a bit strange!' The game was still going on so I was waiting to get him back in the dressing room. I marched in at full time and Billy pushed me into the room and as this guy came in Billy chinned him. Billy looked down at him and said, 'He was going to do that to you, but I've done it on his behalf, because if he'd done it I would have had to suspend him!' Ken Hollyman was a funny little fellow who could wind Billy up. As a player Lucas loved to bring the ball down and play little passes around his own box but he didn't share the same enthusiasm for others doing this and in one game Ken tested his patience to the limit. Billy went at him at half-time and Ken calmly replied 'You used to do it and I am a much better player than you were!' Billy was flabbergasted and said, 'There is bloody no answer to that!'

Some awful form in the latter part of the season was finally averted with a 2-2 draw in the final game at Torquay, eleventh place being just enough to stop the drop into the new basement. Cec Dixon told me,

> Without a doubt the most nervewracking game I ever played for County was the one at Torquay late April 1958. We had to win or at least get a point; it was 'do or die'. We managed to draw so it was virtually like winning promotion. The train trip back to Wales remains in my thoughts forever as it was packed with supporters and a great time was had by all.

Also notable for the season was that on 21 October, County had the distinction of becoming the first Welsh club with floodlights. They were opened with a game against an All Stars XI (lost 4-2) and floodlit friendlies were also enjoyed against European opposition Red Star Olympique of Paris (lost 2-1) and Spandau (won 5-0).

In the first season in the new Third Division, County finished seventeenth, but it was again memorable for a gallant Cup run. Harry Harris was not around this time, however – he had left for Portsmouth in July for a club record £10,000 sale. It was another new face, ex-Marine Ken McPherson, who made headlines this time. There had been no sign of that in the First Round at non-league Wisbech. Only four minutes remained when McPherson saved blushes and just twenty seconds from time in the replay he repeated the feat. After extra time, County cruised through 4-1 and beat Hereford in Round 2 before being drawn home to Torquay. It will pain any self-respecting County fan to know that the 0-0 draw was fought in the blue of Cardiff with borrowed shirts because of a colour clash. It was in the borrowed red shirts of Newport Railways that County won the replay 1-0, again courtesy of McPherson. It was already known that the prize was another glamour tie against the cockerel-crested shirts of Tottenham Hotspur at White Hart Lane! Talking of shirts, County had reverted the strip to the pre-war style of amber with three black hoops, with the intention of removing a hoop each time they were promoted. New signing Les Riggs told me, 'The Chairman, Percy Jones, came in and told us that we would remove one of these when we got promoted to the Second Division. The stitching was too tight though and by the end of the game each of the black bands were literally hanging off, which gave us a good laugh.'

County prepared the day before the Spurs game, in which Bryn Jones would line up against his famous younger brother Cliff, with sherry and eggs. The first half started badly for Weare. Spurs' England striker, the burly Bobby Smith, knocked him into yesterday, and dazed and battered he did well to help keep the score down to 2-0 at half-time. The second half was a totally different proposition. County made light of the gulf in their status and their 5,000-strong following in the 50,561 crowd were in dreamland when Hollyman produced a 30-yard top corner effort in the 64th minute! An equaliser looked inevitable as Spurs were on the ropes, but the one player on the field who would have been well suited to the square ring, Smith, put pay to Wilcox's involvement in the 80th minute, the centre half leaving with a dislocated elbow. That gave Smith the room he needed to score two more and Tottenham won 4-1. The game literally left a mark on Weare, for whom Leicester bid £15,000 during the season, and he told me,

> In those days there was none of this 'leave the 'keeper alone' business you have today and early in the game the England centre-forward Bobby Smith really hammered me and I was in a daze for most of the game. I thought, 'What am I doing and why am I doing this?' I felt that I'd had enough, but next pre-season got back into it. Bill was a good persuader!

County entered the sixties with typical inconsistency. Freely scoring at home, there was nothing to show away and they finished thirteenth. Young Ollie Burton moved on, finding fame with Wales and a long career at Newcastle, winning the 1969 Inter-Cities Fairs Cup. In September at Coventry, boyhood County fan Burton made an unexpected debut, telling me:

> As we were pulling into the ground, a lorry smashed into the front of our coach. Dudley Peake was injured by it and so I played. It was amazing all of a sudden to be in the same dressing room as these people and it served me well. One day,

Sherry and eggs the day before the Spurs game.

Ken Hollyman made me cry and it was the best thing that ever happened to me! We would sometimes mess about in training during five-a-sides. Ken was a bit like a Sergeant Major sticking his chest out and we were losing and he laced into me saying, 'There is more go in a f****** bottle of pop – you are bloody useless boy!' I cried and walked off and he said, 'Come back here' and made me play again. He shook me up, but it taught me a lesson.

However, there was another cup run, and it was Spurs again, this time in the third round at Somerton Park. The following season, Spurs would be the first club to do the double since 1897, so although it was an anticlimax, it was ultimately forgivable to have lost 4-0.

Ken Hollyman and future Norwich, Newcastle and Wales legend Ollie Burton.

Burton stays close to protect Weare from another battering from Spurs No. 9 Bobby Smith.

Some amusing stories have been told to me from that season:
Les Riggs:

Plymouth had a winger making a name for himself so Billy wanted me to make life 'uncomfortable' for him. I had obviously rattled him as when we were walking off the pitch at half-time he came up from behind and clouted me before running off to the safety of the dressing room. I was seething and spent the rest of the second half looking for him, but wherever I went he kept as far away from me as possible. The other Argyle players were laughing, saying, 'There he is', and shouting to their teammate, 'He's behind you!' It was like a panto! The following season he had been transferred to Swindon and in the first few minutes I put him in the stand and out of the game. I ran back to the edge of my box and Alf Sherwood was looking at me bewildered before catching on and saying, 'Oh, I see, Plymouth last season!' 'Yes!' I replied, with a very satisfied smile on my face, I can tell you. In another game the ball hit me hard where I least welcomed it and it completely pole-axed me. I was on the floor and unable to breathe and Alf was the first to come over asking if I was OK. I couldn't even talk, so Alf asked if there was something in my throat, quickly adding, 'for God's sake don't cough, it will be your b******s and you will lose 'em for good!' They pulled me up and I was still bent double when old George Kitson eventually ran on to administer the magic sponge. Trouble was it was so bitterly cold, the contents of his bucket had frozen up and the first I knew of it was a rock hard sponge in my face putting me out for the count and with a bad cut for good measure!

John McSeveney also told me a story concerning Les and Arthur Rowley, the Football League's all-time record goalscorer:

> There was some history between Bill and Arthur, who was at the end of his career at Shrewsbury. Bill offered £10 for someone to 'do him'. That was more than a week's wage, so we were all more than keen when he assured us that he was serious. The first corner came over and Les floored Rowley with a crashing elbow. Les scampered into the dressing room at half-time asking for his tenner, but Billy was having none of it, saying, 'No way ... he got back up!'

The close season was notable for the retirement of Ray Wilcox after 546 appearances. That was softened by a big-name signing – the famed and controversial Wales star, Trevor Ford. Despite his aura, he flopped. Far more successful was another new boy, Granville Smith, who would become a part of the furniture at Somerton for many years. The season's fortunes were decided by the early departure to Birmingham of Jimmy Singer, who had scored nine in nine games, and even more so when Ollie Burton was sold to Norwich for a record £12,000 in January (an

Billy Lucas quit – but would be back!

Ray Wilcox retired from playing but stayed as coach.

Comedian Stan Stennett would sometimes train when his big mate, the famous Trevor Ford, joined.

unhappy Ford also leaving the same day). Singer told me, 'It hurt me but I was practical. I had a wife and child but had to go for the money for the club. I was sad because it had been the best time of my life – lovely people like Alf Sherwood – leaving people like Alf, it hurt.' Burton had starred in more epic cup encounters with Southampton (this time the new League Cup). Two draws saw County in the second replay undo their good work. Burton told me, 'I scored a hat-trick – leading 3-1 with only half an hour left. We lost 5-3! That took the edge off it! You don't expect to score a hat-trick and lose!' Form nosedived. Frustrated, Lucas could do nothing and at the end of the season, again having finished thirteenth, he resigned.

6

DOWN BUT NEVER OUT

County were spoiled for choice in their search to replace Lucas for 1961/62. The failed flirtation with the big name of Ford did not deter applicants, and Celtic, Chelsea and Scotland legend Bobby Evans was announced as player-manager. He prematurely replaced the likes of McPherson, McSeveney, Riggs and Dixon and the retiring Sherwood with fellow Scots, who brought a distinctly north-of-the-border flavour. Despite their eye-catching style of play, they immediately saw the club head south too – to the Fourth Division. The main failure was a lack of goals, although Scottish striker Jock Buchanan told me the blame was with Evans, who had failed to recognise the need to hang up his boots:

I made my debut at home against Grimsby. Len Weare got injured and Bobby went in goal. He thought he could do everything! He lost the plot completely! He would come out with daft ideas and really odd sayings and we would sit there shaking our heads. As a player by then he was slow. His legs had gone. Trouble was, whenever he picked himself to play at centre-half, he would focus all of the blame, if we lost, on the forwards. It was laughable! We got beat four or five nil one game and for the next match he kept the defence as it was and dropped all four forwards! The press were gentle on Bobby, but I think that was because the *Argus* reporter was a bit scared of him! Brentford is the one game I remember. Everything came off for us and for me in particular and we beat them 6-1. In this match it just all clicked. Sometimes you get days like that. We only had the one, but it was one to savour, especially as I scored a hat-trick!

Wilcox was undeservedly sacked as trainer but by mid-March the board were desperate and persuaded Billy Lucas once more to lean on wife Edie to call 'last orders' while he gave them up the road. County finished with twenty-two points – their lowest ever total.

Lucas brought Wilcox back as trainer and put together a prolific strike partnership of Ralph Hunt and Joe Bonson. Laurie Sheffield had also been signed from Barry and between the three of them they scored sixty-nine goals in all competitions, yet it took a final day goal from Hunt to avoid re-election on goal average in a season which, thanks to the 'Big Freeze', saw no games between 22 December and 27 February. Goal average didn't come into it for the two-legged Welsh Cup Final, which County at long last reached after beating Second Division Swansea. The competition would instead be decided on points with a play-off if necessary; but that surely was a formality as County played north Wales minnows Borough United. A goal up at half-time, County returned red faced after losing 2-1 and were left even more upset after the second Leg! Len Weare told me, 'They were only an amateur side playing on the parks. They put the boards up when they played at our place and drew 0-0 and went through to play in Europe. The chairman came in after the game, laid into us and said we were all sacked!' County also reached the third round of the League Cup, going out after losing at home to Manchester City 2-1.

1963/64 was also to be more notable for cup exploits. The season saw the end of greyhound racing and the ground leased from new owners the council, with speedway first making an appearance in April. The loud roar of engines would not have been heard above the sound of 'Cwm Rhondda' in the third round of the Cup, as the crowd were left exhausted by a 3-2 win over Sheffield Wednesday, who were in sixth place in the First Division. Still regarded as one of the greatest nights in the club's history, the 'Owls' went ahead after 19 minutes through England international Eddie Holliday, but Bonson equalised after just three minutes of the second half. County again fell behind, but on sixty-nine minutes a goal kick fell straight to him and he returned it with interest. Just two minutes later, the roof came off as Granville Smith's cross was turned in by Hunt. Weare made a brilliant last-minute save and the biggest scalp in the club's history had been claimed. Wednesday fans had brought a large banner that proclaimed 'Wembley or Bust', and they made their way as one to the exit, all very deliberately and unmistakeably pointing to the word 'Bust'!

It was another First Division outfit in the fourth round – Burnley at Turf Moor. County lost 2-1 but deserved a replay. There was a suspicion of handball for Willie

Weare punches clear from Wednesday's Bronco Layne with Len Hill looking on.

Morgan's goal but the day was a disappointing one for Weare, who told me,

> Our winger, Colin Webster, had the ball and I ran out to him for a back-pass.
> He tried to beat his man though and lost it. The ball was squared and it was an
> easy goal for them. I had stick for that. For their second goal, they had a corner
> and Johnny Bird on the near post ducked and it went in. I had stick for that too!
> It was not a happy game for me. We came back on the train and Director Syd
> Jenkins didn't half lay into Webster in front of fans!

The Welsh Cup ended with a semi-final replay defeat, this time 1-0 to Cardiff
at Ninian Park, County agreeing to play there as the Bluebirds refused to
toss-up for the venue. County finished fifteenth, with Hunt scoring sixteen
while Bonson improved on his previous season's effort with thirty-two.
By any reckoning, that was another excellent return for a partnership that
had amassed an exceptional 107 goals between them in just two seasons.

So County sold them both! How they performed, though, is a wonder, considering what Weare told me:

> I used to live next door to Ralph, who was good mates with Joe and who also lived around the corner. Joe would call on me to walk to the ground for games and we would then get Ralph. I would get to the ground on my own, though, as they would always stop off at the Victoria for a pint first!

Hunt tragically died in a car crash the following December.

Astonishingly, County somehow managed to score a club record eighty-five goals the following season. Sheffield certainly stepped out of their shadows and equalled Hunt's record twenty-seven League goals, but he would be the first to credit the improvement in his supply line through new signing Ken Morgan and young Gil Reece. Morgan had been the youngest of the 'Busby Babes' and the last to be rescued from the wreckage of the Munich Air Disaster. He rediscovered his love of the game under Lucas and this was perfectly demonstrated at home against Lincoln in October. County won 7-0 and Morgan was credited with four goals and another in some quarters which had initially been given as an own goal. I asked him one day if it had been four or five and he answered, 'It was six! I don't know anything about an own goal, as so far as I'm concerned the five I scored were all clear cut; but Granville Smith robbed me of my double hat-trick as he made sure of a goal after my effort had already crossed the line!' Reece had made his debut at the end of 1963/64 and had an outstanding season, showing why he would go on to be awarded twenty-nine Welsh caps. County finished sixteenth and, of course, both Reece and Sheffield were sold.

How could County possibly hope to challenge for promotion when such talent was so quickly sold on? Derek Tapscott, who had been County's undoing in the Arsenal cup tie, was signed, but like Ford he proved his best years were behind him. Another international, Ireland's Alfie Hale, was surprisingly the makeweight in Sheffield's move to Doncaster and it was he who would be the new hero, scoring twenty-four in thirty-eight games. County finished a much improved ninth, thanks to promotion-style form in the last two months. The FA Cup had (for a change) not been a respite, going out 2-0 in the first round at non-league Bath. Injured players that season had every incentive to get fit, as Malcolm Cook, who had joined in the summer, told me:

> A new physio came on the scene – I think his name was Colin and like Lucas he wore a dickey bow and was an endearing character! He cleared out the

treatment room and brought in new ideas, but I don't think he was qualified! He had this electrical thing with a cattle prod and there would be burnt players and sparks flying everywhere! Injuries were at an all time low as no-one would admit to one and risk going in there!

There was great disappointment in the summer when Hale announced he would be returning to Ireland. His £3,000 fee was received in postal orders, coins and stamps. Financial worries were once more to the fore and the side was heavily reliant on local talent. Jeff Thomas, who had actually played as a fifteen-year-old in the Monmouthshire Senior Cup Final, had become the youngest League debutant at sixteen the previous season and he put down his claim to a place in the side. The pounding of the pitch edges through the speedway was beginning to have an impact, and young Jeff was not alone in struggling when it came to taking corners. He told me,

> As an apprentice I used to have to come in on a Saturday morning to re-lay the corners after the speedway and then play in the afternoon! The crowd had a good laugh one day in my first season when I went to take a corner. It was a mess as usual and I was only young and small so it was hard for me to get the ball over. I didn't have the strength! To give myself a bit of a chance I made a tee, a bit like rugby players do. I was busy building the mound up and the ref came over and gave me a rollocking.

It was all too much for Lucas, who in February decided to return to his old club Swansea as manager. Les Graham stepped up from the youth team and in March was joined at the helm by Trevor Morris. They just about steered to safety, finishing eighteenth. 1967/68 got off to a decent start and finished with a respectable twelfth place. Yet again it was the lure of the cup that would keep supporters enthralled, although crowds were worryingly low by the end of the campaign. The League Cup had not been very rewarding, but a second-round game at home to Blackpool attracted a good gate impressed by brave County's 1-0 defeat. Dai Jones had done his best to replace Hale and his form was good enough to bring a bid from Mansfield. He was in turn replaced by Oxford's Tony Buck, who would become hugely popular. Buck's goal at Guildford earned County a third-round tie at old adversaries Southampton. Always a great occasion, the difference now was that Saints were a First Division side. 5,000 County fans went in anticipation of repeating past glories and, 1-0 down, their faith was justified when a penalty was awarded for a foul on the talented Len Hill.

Hill told me what happened next:

Gerald King had been really nervous before the game and when I got pulled down for a penalty, he wasn't too sure about it at all. I said to him, 'Just concentrate and take it.' Gerald ran up and kicked it and his boot came off and went up in the air in the same direction as their 'keeper and the ball went the other side! We could have won, but it was a fair result.

A 17,600 crowd for the replay almost meant a delayed kick-off and did result in the peculiar sight of international stars doing their best to climb a fence, without damaging their expensive suits, to gain access to the ground. By half-time, the experience had not unsettled them as they held a 2-0 lead, but within thirteen minutes of the second half, Alan Williams and Hill had caused a pitch invasion and pulled back on level terms. County were now well on top and a penalty appeal for a foul on Hill was this time not given. Len again took up the story for me:

We should have done even better in the replay, although they had internationals and brilliant wingers like Terry Paine and John Sydenham. I used to veer off into the channels and this was working really well for us. Just as well as David Webb was marking me and trying to break me in half! I was taking him to the cleaners though. Two things cost us the game. We started trying to knock it around at the back like we were Benfica or something, instead of continuing to knock it into the channels for me. Also our full back Joe Wilson clattered Jimmy Gabriel. He went off and young Mick Channon came on. That was the worst thing that could have happened to us! He scored their winner to make it 3-2. He didn't half put it away mind and it stuck in the top stanchion. All three of their goals were cracking that night and struck magnificently back across the way the ball had come to them.

The referee obviously thought it was a goal worthy of winning any game, and blew the full-time whistle early. The traditional Welsh Cup semi-final defeat arrived courtesy of non-league Hereford, with a famous scorer – Albert Derrick. Obviously this was not the pre-war star, but his son, who had been with the club in 1960/61 and would return again before the decade was out. In April, with injuries mounting, Allen Wood, a centre back but capable in just about any position, showed his incredible versatility by playing in goal at Aldershot. He told me,

I walked in to the dressing room to be told I was playing in goal! I can remember they had big Jack Howarth up front and I always had great battles with him. A corner came over and I came out to catch it, but he beat me to it and his header hit the bar and came straight back to my arms! They knocked a ball over the top and I came out calling for it, but Alan Smith knocked it past me and they scored.

Allen thought the game had ended 1-0 and laughed upon discovering it was in fact a 2-0 defeat:

Really? I can't remember a second goal. Maybe I didn't see it at the time! I do remember feeling proud of myself making a diving save – but when I looked back I was at least 4 yards outside the posts, so there was no need!

County finished twelfth. Little could supporters have realised that the next few years would be severely depressing. 1968/69 began with the lowest opening gate for thirty-seven years and no goals in the first five games. The only high point of the season was Tony Buck scoring all five in the 5-1 win at Bradford PA. Money worries predominated and fundraisers were played against Plymouth and Cardiff. In February, the decision was taken to cash in on Buck, who was sold to Rochdale for £5,000. The club had changed strip to tangerine and white, but no change in fortune came with that. Steve Aizlewood, who lived a stone's throw from the ground, was given permission to have a day off school and play at Chesterfield. He told me, 'On my debut they all disappeared and I found they'd gone to the bookies. Les Graham even gave me a tip!' Little wonder Graham was sacked before the final match and County had to face re-election. They succeeded, but with a stiff warning, particularly as the ground was not of the standard required.

John Rowland had been granted a testimonial against Portsmouth and left for Barry after 531 appearances, during which he had set a record for consecutive appearances. Cardiff's Bobby Ferguson joined as player-manager and introduced new faces including locals Martyn Sprague, skilful left-winger Andy White and ultra wholehearted (and future Hall of Famer) Roddy Jones, who despite always being a part-time pro would become one of the club's most popular figures, giving equally wonderful service at the back or up front. All three would perform admirably for County, but it would take a time for their influence to be felt. This season would instead end with another re-election and the final game against Grimsby was played in front of an all-time low crowd of 1,009. New mascot 'Tangerine Tommy', the brainchild of super-fan and future director and programme editor Ray Taylor, had not brought luck and Ray Wilcox must have given him a rue look on the way out as he was sacked after thirty-one years' service. County even enlisted 'The Voice' – Tom Jones, who the previous season had become club president, gave a concert to raise much-needed funds. Typical County – by the time even this superstar had taken his expenses, County were out of pocket. However, a fundraising drive had enabled Graham Coldrick to be bought from Cardiff for £4,000. Sadly, the season was to be Len Weare's last, retiring after fifteen years and 607 games, during which shamefully he was never granted a testimonial. At last, though, County found a worthy successor in John Macey.

And it was to get worse before it got better. In 1970/71, County made an all-out assault on the record for the most games before recording a win. It took ten games to earn a point and their twenty-sixth before Southend were overcome on 15 January, Billy Lucas' birthday. That was special, as by then Lucas had been once more tempted from behind his bar as Ferguson had been relieved of his managerial duties after another record-breaking day – the highest

John 'Polly' Rowland made 531 appearances between 1958 and 1969.

score for a League team to lose to non-league opponents in the FA Cup. Barnet won 6-1 and that was all the humiliation anyone could bear. Aizlewood told me,

> We'd had a scouting report which said about Ricky George to just show him inside. We did that to him twice early in the game and boomp boomp he scored twice! We could have scored more as well but everything they hit flew in.

John Macey added,

> For one of their goals, I shouted for the ball, but Fergie just headed it past me! He went mad in the dressing room after the game. There were bottles of Schweppes on a tray and he came in and swept them off. The glass went all over the bath area and no one could have a shower. We had a very young side and it was a combination of this and not playing together as a team that caused us such problems.

Jeff Thomas winced as he recalled, 'My mother was shouting "rubbish!" When your mum shouts "rubbish" then you've got no chance!' In 1972, Ronnie Radford and Ricky George would cause one of the greatest FA Cup shocks of all time when Hereford beat Newcastle. He won the Player of the Year and had no doubt about the reason for the change in form after that first win, telling me,

> Getting that under our belt did more for us than anything anyone specifically did differently. The belief came back. The tension was terrible until we won and that really lifted us. It is amazing what one result can do. People had been frightened of making mistakes and that becomes a habit. Winning creates a good habit and as a unit you perform and it quickly spreads throughout the team. You have to stay focussed but remain relaxed and avoid the fear factor, which is incredibly hard when you go as many games without winning as we did! We then had some really good performances, especially beating Notts County, who were running away with the League. We also drew with Bournemouth, who were also flying and had Ted MacDougall scoring goals for fun.

Lucas had said when taking over, 'If we are to die as a Football League club, let us die honourably and with dignity.' He performed wonders, winning the Manager of the Month in March and although it was too late to avoid a third successive re-election, the improvement had won admiration and friends and a final execution order was stayed.

Billy Lucas wins Manager of the Month.

Lucas knew 1971/72 was the last-chance saloon and persuaded the board to bring in the vastly experienced Everton and Cardiff captain Brian Harris as a player coach, later upgraded to assistant manager. His position, alongside Aizlewood, had been freed up by the shock signing of John Saunders by Don Revie's Leeds. However, by April things were again bleak and re-election beckoned. On Easter Tuesday it all clicked, winning 4-0 against Darlington with Andy White even scoring direct from a corner. Promotion form followed and success was guaranteed in dramatic style at Stockport. Losing 3-0 after sixty-five minutes, County scored two in the last two minutes to draw 4-4. One day in the season will never be forgotten. Against Brentford, the club was persuaded to try new shorts. Aizlewood told me,

> We had to wear these ridiculous tangerine and black striped shorts that made us look like minstrels! I always went out second. 'Codgie' (Graham Coldrick) was captain and as we got to the end of the tunnel I stopped and he went out on his own to wolf whistles from the crowd!

Two new signings made a big impact in 1972/73 – Willie Screen and Bob Summerhayes. The foundations had been laid in that end of season run-in and for a change County kept up the momentum in what was the greatest, but ultimately most heartbreaking, season since the war. The first opening game point in five years was earned at Gillingham and that promise was followed by beating Chester at home 3-2. Their young left back had endured a mixed afternoon, having turned in an Andy White cross past his own 'keeper and later spectacularly curling one over Macey from out wide. His name was John Relish, but more of him later. In between, County had gone to Third Division Swansea in the League Cup and, although pegged back with a last-minute equaliser, won the replay 3-0 with Willie Brown scoring a hat-trick. The iconic Brown, who had been signed in 1970 with money raised by the Supporters' Club, was to form a potent partnership with Roddy Jones that would keep County in the promotion race all season. First Division Ipswich, managed by Bobby Robson with Bobby Ferguson as his assistant, were too strong and won the second-round tie at Somerton 3-0. County's toughest opponent in the early part of the season seemed to be the railway. At both Colchester and Exeter County arrived late, but still came away with a win and a draw. Some outstanding performances included doing the double over bogey team Aldershot and that season's champions Southport; 5-1 home wins over Hartlepool and Gillingham; and the same score at Doncaster. Brown repeated

Above: The 1970/71 squad pre-season. They recovered magnificently after a traumatic start.

Left: The legendary Roddy Jones.

his hat-trick after bringing Swansea back for another replay, this time in the Welsh Cup, and all were headers. That brought Second Division Cardiff in the next round and a below-par 3-1 defeat. However, the season was marred by struggling against lesser sides and in particular a number of missed penalties. Hereford, on the back of their cup exploits, had replaced Barrow and won 1-0 at Somerton in a game appallingly refereed by controversial the John Yates – a former 'Bulls' player. At Easter, their Edgar Street ground was at capacity as they won again, this time by 2-0.

This was to prove crucial, although it all came down to the last game – almost. In the week before, having beaten Workington, all awaited the results elsewhere in the hope that Aldershot had beaten Cambridge or vice versa. If so, County would have to beat Bury on Saturday to go up. Of course, it was a draw. Now not only would County have to beat the 'Shakers' but also rely on any of the following: Cambridge and Mansfield to draw, the highly unlikely scenario of Hereford losing to re-election threatened Crewe, or Aldershot losing at Stockport the following Friday.

Somerton had never been so tense, but an early Coldrick penalty settled nerves. At half-time Cambridge and Mansfield were drawing 2-2. Bury equalised, but goals from Aizlewood and Jones had County 3-1 up as the game was closing down. County traditionally kicked off fifteen minutes later than most clubs and everyone in the 7, 390 crowd (it seemed much larger!) was seeking updates from those with transistor radios. Then, in a tragically comic way befitting only of County, the BBC announced that Hereford had lost 1-0. There was pandemonium – two goals to the good County would surely see out the remaining ten minutes! The news quickly reached the players, and concentration was lost. Bury scored again before Dai Jones made it 4-2 with a wonderful solo effort. Bury then scored what looked an offside goal to make it 4-3. The whistle blew – supporters and players celebrated wildly. The press box didn't – they knew the truth was that Hereford had in fact won.

Cambridge also beat Mansfield 3-2, so it was a long wait until Friday. Graham Coldrick told me,

> Bury had been offered a few bob to beat us. I scored the first – another penalty. Steve Aizlewood said to me, 'If you don't want to take it, I will.' My heart was in my mouth! I got back to the dressing room thinking we were up – we were gutted!

Graham's wife, June, added:

Some of us lived close to each other and all the wives were out dancing in the street. We'd already opened the champagne and were all half cut – and then later on John Macey's wife knocked the door and said we weren't up!

Aldershot got the point they need at Stockport with a second-half equaliser and it was future County legend Richard Walden celebrating and not County, who had lost out by the slimmest goal average difference of 0.12.

So close but yet so far, County splashed out as favourites for promotion in 1973/74 with the club record signing of Brian Godfrey for £10,000. His Bristol Rovers teammate, veteran Harold Jarman, also joined but the season finished a desperately disappointing ninth. Harris had replaced Lucas as manager in January, with Bill moving upstairs as General Manager. Len Hill told me,

We should have gone on, but we made some bad buys. We didn't need to sign Brian Godfrey. It hurt Bob Summerhayes and he came up to me and said, 'We did ok last season didn't we?' Godfrey would go forward where Bob would sit in and be a lynchpin for us, so the balance was disturbed. We also signed Harold Jarman on the wing. He was alright but too old and not the answer. If a signing was needed it was up front. No disrespect to Roddy or Willie, but it is the hardest place to play and you need more competition for places up there.

For 1974/75, John Relish was signed from Chester. Also here now was Bobby Woodruff and striker Eddie Woods, who came in initially on loan and made a great impression. However, despite the nucleus of the side remaining and some quality additions, things never seemed to quite gel in the same way. County ended up twelfth, with the highlight being a courageous 4-2 League Cup defeat at Chelsea, who triumphed through a Chris Garland hat-trick, but more especially the brilliance of winger Charlie Cooke. Woodruff scored the goal of the game with a 30-yard top corner screamer. Roddy Jones told me,

It was possibly the first time that their new main stand was used for a night time match, although we had to get changed in portakabins. I had a particularly good game that day and can remember their manager Dave Sexton coming up to me after and saying, 'Well played son.' That was fantastic for me to have someone of his stature in the game coming up and saying that to me. They were full of stars and Charlie Cooke did a shimmy and the whole stand moved! I gave Micky Droy, who I can remember looking up at because he was so huge, and Ron 'Chopper' Harris a real battering that night. Probably my best 'goal' was in that game – or it would have been had it not been disallowed by 1974 World Cup referee Jack Taylor, for Brownie being offside. It would have been allowed today as he was out on the wing and not interfering with play.

A 4-3 defeat at home to Barnsley in March saw the dejected Harris resign, infamously being quoted that the people of Newport were interested in only 'betting, booze and bingo'. Lucas of course popped into the hot seat as caretaker and hopefully took some comfort from the reserves under Granville Smith winning the Welsh League. The youth team was also showing exceptional promise and they beat Chelsea away in the FA Youth Cup.

Former Newcastle player Dave Elliott was appointed player-manager for 1975/76, starting with a 3-1 win at home against future England manager Graham Taylor's Lincoln. That was all the more outstanding given the 'Imps' broke all kind of records that season, and when I had dinner with Taylor years later it was notable how much that blemish still rankled him. The following game was also won – the first two opening game victories since 1934 – but there was little else to cheer, only nails to bite, as re-election loomed again. At Doncaster, five goals were conceded in an incredible six minutes. In February, Elliott was sacked and replaced by Jimmy Scoular, scourge of County for Pompey in the 1948/49 Cup encounter and who had enjoyed great success as manager of Cardiff. He had been out of the game for two years but was still respected, which is why County were re-elected. Steve Aizlewood was sold and the circumstances tell you much about County's mismanagement, as he explained to me:

A deal was all set up to sell me to Cardiff for £25,000 and Gary Bell and Don Murray, but chairman Cyril Rogers knocked it on the head as he wanted more money. It was the bank who then actually sold me – to Swindon for £13,500 and then County went out and bought Bell and Murray!

One positive was the outstanding youth team, which reached the later stages of the FA Youth Cup, won the Welsh Youth Cup and produced some big names: Steve's brother Mark, Nigel Vaughan and Steve Lowndes, all of who would become full Internationals. Relish broke his leg, although he enjoyed himself at Huddersfield when the teams were introduced to his political hero Prime Minister, Harold Wilson. Relish told me, 'Roddy Jones reckons I bowed to him! Cyril Rogers, doing the presentations, forgot Roddy's name. Roddy said, "It's okay chairman, I've only been here nine years!"'

John Macey, a worthy successor to Weare, and Steve Aizlewood had both left by the end of 1975/76.

Above: County, Liverpool and Ireland legend John 'Ollie' Aldridge with Andrew and Angela Taylor.

Below: Match programme from 5-1 defeat at Millwall, 6 October 1919.

The only known photograph from County's first Football League season in 1920/21, which saw the stripes play the reds in the traditional pre-season trial game.

County pictured before the 4-1 demolition of Swansea in April 1924.

Left: Harold Williams.

Right: Stanley Matthews at the All Star game in 1955.

Below: Public celebration of the 1979/80 'Double'.

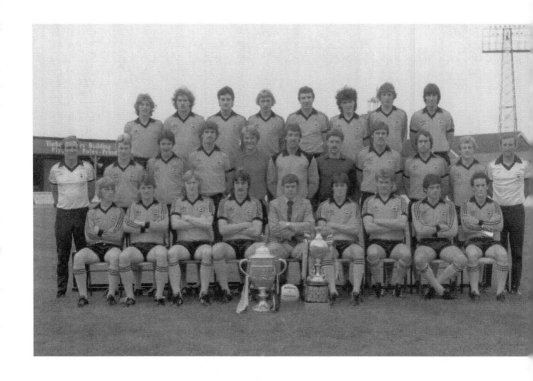

Above: The 1980/81 side not only show the Welsh Cup and Welsh League Championship trophy, but are about to amaze Europe!

Below: Tommy Tynan, County's most iconic hero.

Twenty-fifth European Cup Winners' Cup Anniversary Reunion. *From left*: Lowndes, Oakes, Goodfellow, Plumley, Relish, Dowler, Kendall, Davies, Warriner, Ward, Elsey and Vaughan, with Andrew Taylor the only one still able to kneel!

Directors, management and squad line up for the historic first Hellenic game v. Pegasus Juniors.

David Jarvis scores at Edgar Street but now it is in the Hellenic against Pegasus and not Hereford!

Chris Lilygreen in AFC's first season Cup final.

Graham Rogers leads out a triumphant return to Somerton Park as Hellenic League champions.

Jason Prew scores the last competitive goal at Somerton Park before heading back to exile.

'End of an era', 22 July 1993, the remains of Somerton Park closes with a Past v. Present game.

Guppy scores a late winner against Peter Nicholas' Llanelli to win the 2007/08 FAW Premier Cup. County were the last winners of this televised competition as the BBC cancelled its sponsorship.

The Conference South Trophy is presented at the Dover game as County are crowned champions!

Taking in the first ever Wembley experience at the FA Trophy final.

Left: Manager Justin
Edinburgh keeps County
up and gets to Wembley
for the Trophy final –
what a start!

Below: The first game at
the new ground versus
Bristol Rovers.

New signing Christian Jolley had major influence on promotion back to the League.

Not even smoke in his eyes would distract Lenny Pidgeley in magnificent form at Grimsby in the play-off first leg.

Celebrating another 'Jolley good goal' at home against Grimsby in the second leg.

Forget the venue, Wembley becomes Little Wales, but is irrelevant this time as the only thing that matters is the result as County prepare for the most importan ninety minutes of their history.

Former Youth product Mike Flynn knew what it meant to fans as he takes the game to Wrexham.

County survive as Wrexham miss!

Jolley unleashes a million Welsh tears to make it 1-0 four minutes from time ...

... and he celebrates with the delirious County faithful.

In the last minute of injury time, O'Connor seals promotion.

County players and staff celebrate

'It's there – 2-0 – County are up! Its 2-0 – we are back in the Football League after 25 years! The referee looks at his watch – there it is – County are back!' Tim Thraves, Newport City Radio.

Les Scadding (*front left*) is jubilant as David Pipe tries not to drop the trophy, with former chairmen John Williams and David Hando looking on.

The banner gives confirmation.

The legends who made it 'mission accomplished' giving Newport County AFC the 'ultimate season of triumph.' May the next 100 years be twice as successful and half as stressful!

7

ESCAPE TO VICTORY

There was disbelief as much as anger when Scoular's first act of 1976/77 was to change the colours to blue-and-white stripes. Kick-off was also brought in line to 3 p.m. He made some exciting signings, even if most were at the end of their careers, trying to relive his glory days at Cardiff with the likes of Brian Clark and Steve Derrett joining other ex-Bluebirds. At the other end of the scale was outstanding young 'keeper Gary Plumley from Leicester. They ended up giving excellent service, but for much of the season, rather than emulating Argentina, results were little better than had Afan Lido replaced them in the League. The season was to prove one of the most difficult yet exhilarating in the club's history, forever being known as 'The Great Escape'.

For all Scoular's legendary playing success and his management triumphs at Cardiff (during which, with a number of this side, they famously beat Real Madrid), he was now something of a caricature from a bygone era. Possibly the toughest player of his generation and still with a temper to match, he was also a superbly technical footballer, as Nigel Vaughan noted one day, telling me,

The ex-Cardiff boys knew how to wind him up. They'd knock the ball in five-a-sides just so he had to stretch and watch him moan. We'd play left footers v. right and he would go mad with his own side – we'd never finish until they'd won! But I will always remember he had us practicing pattern play with the ball going from right back to centre midfield and then out to Andy White on the left wing. They couldn't do it and he lost patience, got hold of the ball and immediately drilled it 60 yards straight to Andy's feet. He didn't have to move! From that point on I looked at him as a different bloke.

John Relish added,

> Oh God, Scoular frightened the life out of me! He was no more than 5 ft
> 8 inches but was a giant of a character and from a different era altogether.
> He was tough but fantastically loyal to his players. He would crucify you
> one-to-one but never let anyone else do so. In training he would kick
> everyone – he would top you! You couldn't row with him as if you did he'd
> say, 'We'll go to Spytty and sort it out man to man!'

For all his faults he was incredibly hardworking, even down to refitting the
dressing rooms himself and repainting the lines on the pitch. He also gave rise
to many amusing stories, including the one told me by 'keeper Mike Dowler:

> He had this saying, in that gruff Scottish accent of his, if you didn't spot the
> chance to switch the ball to the other side, 'Christ son, have you only one eye!'
> We were in a pre-season friendly and Mark Williams gave the ball away when
> someone had made a run the other side. He shouted it out as usual and the
> nearest opposition player turned around – and he had a glass eye!

The season began poorly. The style of play was attractive enough, but points
were hard to come by. New boy Plumley was outstanding and so defeats were
narrow, but by October the club was in crisis and looking very unlikely to see
the season out.

Supporters did their best to raise money, with five walking to the cup game
at Southend, and football showed its caring side with Dave Mackay and Des
Anderson both donating large newspaper fees and First Division Coventry
playing a friendly. Just County's luck, it was torrential rain and affected
the crowd, who were perhaps fortunate to miss seeing the visitors score
seven. Cardiff's manager came up with the idea of a South Wales XI playing
Manchester United. Supporters were frustrated to only see Clark, Murray and
Plumley feature, but it was a lifeline, raising £8,000. Even if the money could
be found to limp across the line, County looked doomed. There was little point
in even preparing a re-election brochure, everyone accepting that this would be
once too often. In January, Scoular resigned and was replaced by Colin Addison,
who had masterminded Hereford's ascent from non-league. His impact off the
field was immediate, recognising County had to be out in the community and
working tirelessly alongside commercial manager Mike Lewis, but it took a few
games to be felt where it more immediately mattered. But when it did, it was the

New strip, new faces, 1976/77. *From left*: Trainer Ronnie Bird, Mark Williams, Gary Plumley, John Emanuel, Brian Clark, Ron Walker, Tony Villars and Steve Derrett.

In a side packed with experience, young 'keeper Plumley carried off the Player of the Year award. After one exceptional performance, the vastly experienced Don Murray (*end right*) told Plumley, 'You've just added value to your transfer fee mate - you've gone up a tenner!'

stuff of legend. He made some astute signings in Brian Preece and Tony Byrne from his old club and Dave Bruton on loan from Swansea. Beating Southport 3-1 on 4 March heralded a change in form that was more impressive than even in 1970/71. Top of the table Cambridge, managed by Addison's close friend Ron Atkinson, were overwhelmed 4-2, but by the final five games, four of which were at home, it still remained a surely insurmountable task as County would need to win all five to stand a chance of avoiding the drop. Three games in and Southend beaten 3-0, supporters were daring to believe in the impossible and there were ecstatic scenes as the crowd surged onto the pitch and remained around the players' tunnel. Two games remaining were away and home to Workington, and they were also deeply in trouble. It was now clear, despite the formalities of re-election, that it was winner takes all and the loser would end their League days.

Addison talked to me about that period:

There wasn't plenty to do, there was everything to do! After a month, Mike Lewis said, 'Do me a favour', and took me to Ringland knocking on doors. People were throwing coins in the bucket. I will never forget it. Little Brian Preece scored a great volley to win at Workington and we had a few pints. Then of course on the Monday night we had to go again. I would be the first off the coach at Ross-on-Wye. I turned the radio off and said, 'This is it now – we've not come through all this to fail – see you Monday!' We went from 1,000 in my first game to 8,000 on the last day of the season. I drove down from Hereford thinking, 'We ain't gonna fail!' I'd done it at Hereford under pressure in the last game when we went up and I wasn't going to let it go now.

The programme cover featured Ron Walker and Roddy Jones holding a superimposed banner proclaiming 'The Great Escape' and Eddie Woods' famous winner made this a reality, giving Addison one of his favourite moments in football. 'I will never forget it, it was May the 17th and I left Paddy's Bar at ten past twelve and it was now my birthday. It was a wonderfully satisfying feeling!' Woods told me:

About two to three games left I really began to believe we could do it. We had to beat Workington in the last game and I scored, although it was not exactly the best goal of my career! Addo got us to go up into the stand at the end of the game to thank the crowd. It was packed out there, and the supporters gathered on the pitch as we threw our shirts to them. Great scenes!

Right: Inspirational ex-Arsenal, Nottingham Forest and Sheffield United star Addison shows the way in training.

Below: Unbridled relief and joy as Eddie Woods completes the Escape by scoring one of the most crucial goals in County's history and consigning Workington to the wilderness.

Addison brought back Bill Lucas, the man who called everyone 'matey', as youth adviser and, shrewdly in tune with the views on the terraces, told me about a board meeting towards the end of the season:

> Director Archie Menzies asked me if it would be possible to change colours next season, saying 'I've never been an Argentina supporter and would like him to consider going back to amber and black.' There was a brief pause and I replied, 'That is not a problem – I hate that strip. Newport County are amber and black! And I'll tell you another thing as well – we will kick off again at 3.15 p.m. – we still have shift workers at Llanwern so we do that for the supporters!' It was not about scoring brownie points – that was Newport County!

There was a real buzz around the town and the good feeling continued as County were genuine promotion contenders in 1977/78, strengthened by the signing of the exceptional striking talent Howard Goddard. The only fly in the ointment was the inevitable constant linking of Addison with other jobs. Swansea were persistent and Addison told me,

> It was a brilliant offer and much more money. I rang back and said, 'Look it's a great offer, a big club and great potential, but no thanks', and they improved the offer, which would have made me the highest paid manager in the Division! I said no again. Of course John Toshack got it then and took them all the way up to the First Division, but I just felt that it wasn't right. I had it all going for me at Newport. I didn't say it at the time, but just thought I may just get County up.

There was change of chairman, with Richard Ford replacing Ron Warry, and by December County were fourth and crowds were flooding back. This would be too good a story to continue, so in true County fashion, injuries struck and the final ten games saw County drop from fourth to seventeenth. It was so bad that 1960s' star Mike McLaughlin was tempted away from his current pastime – playing rugby for Newport Saracens. McLaughlin told me,

> Addo came to watch me up the Valleys playing for the Sarries on a night when the ball wasn't really a part of the game! He said, 'I thought you were crazy – now I know you are absolutely nuts!' I was hearing whispers that he wanted me to come back. I ended up ringing his wife and she told me it was true, but he knew I was happy at Sarries and didn't want to disturb me. So I rang him and

he told me he wanted me to get to Stockport on Friday night. I got the impression the players thought I was just coming to watch!

In May came the news fans dreaded. Addison had finally been tempted away and joined First Division West Brom as assistant to Ron Atkinson. The month before, eighteen-year-old Aizlewood had become the club's record sale at £50,000 to Luton and so fans could be forgiven for thinking 'here we go again!' There was no sense of excitement at the announcement of ex-Sunderland star Len Ashurst as his replacement. Had fans learned nothing since similar mutterings when Kelso left the club in 1938? County were about to embark on the most golden years of their history.

Ashurst had been out of work for nine months after being sacked by Sheffield Wednesday. He quietly started to make signings that would form the backbone of the success to come. The faultless Richard Walden would be referred to by his teammates as 'Rolls Royce', and supposedly in the twilight of his career was a bargain from Wednesday with his £3,500 fee decided by the first ever transfer tribunal being well below Jack Charlton's £20,000 valuation. Ashurst told me, 'Jack didn't even attend. I did and I believe that my personally putting the case swayed the panel in our favour whereas, Jack could not be bothered and it went against them. What a wonderful bit of business that was!' Grant Davies and Neil Bailey were signed beginning to form a north-west contingent whose togetherness with the local boys would be a key factor, although it was an awful start ,with six of the first seven lost. In September, Keith Oakes became a record £15,000 buy from Peterborough and would be popularly acclaimed as County's all time best centre-half and captain. The surrounds of his signing did not suggest County were breaking the bank, Oakes telling me, 'The secretary, Phil Dauncey, picked me up at Newport station and took me for a slap up meal at Wimpy's. When we walked towards the ground I thought, "Oh dear!" I'd seen better!' His fee was quickly broken by paying £17,500 to bring back Dave Bruton. Youth products Lowndes and Vaughan emerged. In January, County made up for the relative lack of recent FA Cup entertainment by reaching the third round for the first time since 1973, and it was a glamour tie with a West Ham side including the likes of Trevor Brooking and Billy Bonds. Even now, all fans know County won 2-1. Goddard opened the scoring, 'Pop' Robson scored a superb long-range effort to equalise and Eddie Woods took the roof off with the winner.

Most of that side have shared their memories of that night with me and a few are repeated here. Young Nigel Vaughan was given a boost before the game:

Star-studded West Ham cannot cope with Keith Oakes.

We went to the New Inn and West Ham were there. I was in the back of a car with Eddie Woods and he turned around and said, 'Did you hear that, Vaughnie?' Trevor Brooking said, 'I hope Nigel Vaughan isn't playing!' I was so pleased with the first goal as we had worked on our corners.

Gary Plumley:

We played West Ham on the beach! The first game was called off because of a frozen pitch and so they covered it in sand for the Tuesday night and I don't know who ordered it, but after that there was no grass left on it! As the pitch recovered, because it was dredging sand, the salt in it killed the grass. After that, when you walked on it, you could smell the sea! On the pitch before the game we could see the West Ham bus come over Somerton Bridge and Tony Byrne said, '1-0! That's it 1-0 – they've taken one look at the pitch and said what the hell was that!' One thing that sticks out for me was that I saved a header from David Cross in the second half and him looking at me and shaking his head.

Howard Goddard:

Len Ashurst got up to every trick in the book to psyche them out. They had no soap in the dressing room and it was bloody freezing, but we kept their heating right down! He arranged for the floodlights to not be on properly for the first 10 minutes so they were dazzled and also pumped all of their practice balls up extra hard! Their manager John Lyall came in and said 'Len don't you have any better balls?' – Len just looked at him and said 'This is Divison Four – You're lucky to have a ball!' Their faces when they ran out were a picture – Trevor Brooking, Frank Lampard, all of them – you could see them thinking 'what the hell is this?' I went past Billy Bonds in the first 5 minutes and he came up to me and said 'I'm going to break your f*****g legs.' I laughed at him and said, 'You've got to f******g catch me first!' He didn't catch me though because I scored after about 12 minutes. It was a great thing for the club – the hype was amazing.

John Relish confirmed:

Len did everything possible to make it unpleasant for them. I can remember Billy Bonds before the game walking gingerly in his white shoes! Len warned me about Trevor Brooking's 'trick' where he dropped his shoulder. After 2 minutes, the ball was played in to him and he 'did me' with his trick and as I'm charging back after him all I could see was Len with his head in his hands!

Grant Davies:

The atmosphere was absolutely tremendous. 'Pop' Robson did me like a kipper to score for them. The ball was knocked into his feet and I turned like the Titanic and got a fair bit of stick from my colleagues for that! He made me look stupid but hit a shot that probably nobody would have stopped. At the end we thought to ourselves, 'We are giant-killers!' Then we had a bit of complacency and lost to Ton Pentre in the Welsh Cup! Len went ape about that!

Match-winner Eddie Woods:

Frank Lampard was pinning me down when the corner came across to me for my goal. It went over their 'keeper Mervyn Day, but fortunately I was holding onto the far post at the time – if I hadn't have been then Lampard would have had more leverage to come across me, but I was able to hold my position and the ball rolled down my chest and in.

Irish international Tony Byrne, who had seen it all in the First Division, was the only one with a tinge of disappointment, cheekily adding, 'I was disappointed because I wanted to go to London!' Colchester were at Somerton for the fourth round and a drab goalless draw was followed by a 1-0 replay defeat, which was all the more heartbreaking as at stake was a home tie against Manchester United.

Buoyed by the success in February, Tommy Tynan, arguably the club's most iconic star, was signed for a club record £25,000 along with another club legend, left winger Kevin Moore from Swansea. Truth be told, Tynan was not an instant hit, but the season finished an encouraging eighth and with a record nine away wins. Even so, the 1979/80 'Season of Triumph' surpassed all expectations. A boost was received by Ashurst turning down a return to Sunderland, and the opening game at home to Port Vale was the first time there was no new face in the line up since 1963. In April, though, a south Liverpool hopeful recommended by Ashurst's brother Robin had slipped in unnoticed for only £3,500. His initial impact had not exactly been what he had hoped for when at twenty-one he was given the chance he believed had passed him by to join a League club. His name was John Aldridge, and he told me,

I was terribly homesick and ready to jack it all in, especially after a pre-season game in Cwmbran – I just wanted to go home! I was crap in my first game too – in the reserves at Llanelli. I can remember Brian Clark trying to get my chin up after the game, but a while later he admitted that he'd wondered what the hell they'd signed!

Aldridge made his debut home to Lincoln at the end of September and scored his first two against Aldershot in a 4-2 win shortly after, setting County on a nice little run. Portsmouth away was a big occasion not just because of the history, but their crowds were very large by Fourth Division standards. 20,750 saw County come away with a 2-0 win but few were smiling. Howard Goddard, who had been top scorer in both his seasons, was as usual on fire and already leading the scoring chart. His irrepressible energy was also creating chances for others but tragedy struck when he broke his leg during the game. History shows that Aldridge would come in and indisputably make his own name, and years later many would say that Goddard's tragedy (although he played in to his thirties, he never made an impression again for County after a long recovery) was Aldridge's good fortune. Indeed, some feel that such was Goddard and Tynan's ability, Aldridge may never have progressed. The truth was that it would have been Goddard's last game in any event, as Ashurst told me:

> Just two days before that game I took a call from David Pleat who was manager of Luton at that time. He wanted to sign Howard and we agreed a good price of £100,000. Pleat was going to Pompey to watch the game and he would have signed him the next day. We knew it was a bad break as you could hear it in the stand! Pleat went past me looking quite upset and shrugged and said, 'Sorry Len.'

Goddard added,

> We were winning 1-0 and ripping them apart. Steve Davey came on for them at half-time and done me good and proper – he went in two-footed over the ball and I got done – simple as that.

But Steve Aizlewood, of all people, who had played with Goddard at Swindon, was now Pompey captain and saw it differently, telling me:

> It was just in front of me. Kevin Moore had done my ligaments and I was sat in the dug-out when Steve Davey broke his leg in a tackle. There was no malice – it was a centre-forward playing centre-half. I limped over and said, 'Howard, sit still!' His leg was all over the place – it was a really horrible break.

Just two weeks later, Pompey came to Somerton seeking revenge in a game that left the 7,115 crowd breathless. Regarded as one of the greatest League encounters ever seen at Somerton, the score swayed – 1-0, 1-1, 1-2, 2-2, 3-2, 3-3 – until finally decided by Tynan's second of the night. Aldridge was certainly taking his chances and he scored his first hat-trick at Stockport with County equalling their best ever away score of 5-0. Tynan, though, despite his starring role against Pompey, was generally not living up to his billing and looked likely to trail centre-half Oakes, who was equally adept at either end of the park, in the scoring chart. The pressure on him increased in December when Dave Gwyther became the new record signing at £40,000, but he was struck by injury after just fourteen minutes. Ashurst experimented and played Tynan in a deep lying role; his intelligent play enabled him to rediscover his touch and confidence and he became the greatest of terrace favourites. His claim was staked when, on as sub, his last-minute header helped beat Second

Division Cardiff in the Welsh Cup 2-0 – the first success over their rivals since 1940. The next round was Second Division Wrexham away – there would be no easy route to the final this year! League form had stuttered and so this was where most hopes now rested. Gwyther was now fit and partnering Aldridge, Dave Bruton had added his presence to midfield and Davies was a speedy complement to Oakes. At Tranmere the match announcer drew applause struggling to deal with the changes prior to kick-off, but the applause from the travelling fans at the end of a 2-0 win was to become commonplace. County had begun a record-breaking run of ten consecutive League wins broken only by an Oakes own goal in a 1-1 draw at Darlington. Early in that run Wrexham had also been knocked out of the Cup by a Lowndes goal. Merthyr at home was the kind semi-final draw, and if Shrewsbury could beat Swansea in the other game, the incentive was not just an appearance in the final, but automatic qualification for Europe. Keith Oakes was named in the Fourth Division All Star side and was now the highest scoring defender in the entire Football League.

The Swansea semi-final kicked off fifteen minutes later than County's. The name 'Ton Pentre' was posted in the dressing room as an ominous reminder and a screamer from Gwyther, already a favourite with six goals in as many games, settled it 3-1. I vividly recall remaining seated in the lower section of the stand while the PA system relayed events at Swansea, who were 2-1 up. The biggest cheer of the night was for Shrewsbury's equaliser and there was last-minute confusion if the 'Shrews' had won, but it was cleared and there was to be a three-week wait to discover who the final opponents would be. During this run, County bought Somerton Park from the borough council. The final of the consecutive wins was at home to Rochdale. Late in the game, a voice from County's bench shouted, 'Keep it in their area.' Rochdale's manager Bob Stokoe, who had famously guided Sunderland to their famous FA Cup Final win over Leeds, shouted back, 'Keep it in your own area. It'll be safer there!' County were third with just five games remaining. Shrewsbury beat Swansea on penalties, with the Swans' Alan Waddle shooting skywards to put County in Europe! Relish admitted, 'We had some celebration that night,' which perhaps explained why the record-breaking win sequence ended the next day. That was followed by a shock 3-0 loss at Bradford, but the following Saturday home to Hartlepool was reminiscent of 1972/73, with a combination of results needed to gain promotion. Walsall and Huddersfield were already promoted and if Portsmouth lost at home and County won then the long wait was over. Pompey took a 2-0 lead and County missed a penalty, but early in the second half the winner came courtesy of Aldridge arriving at breakneck speed to head home. County now needed two points from their final two games, both away, and they could not be a greater contrast – bottom side Rochdale on Tuesday and champions-elect Walsall on the final Saturday! What happened next I will relate as described to me by the heroes themselves.

Len Ashurst has painful memories of the Rochdale game, which saw a shock 2-0 defeat and a large Newport contingent returning home feeling that once again it would not be their year.

> That was the ultimate 'double-whammy' that night. I can't recollect a thing about the game except that the referee was awful. After the game, the Rochdale secretary came up to me and took me aside. There was a phone call from my brother saying that our beloved father had died that day. Everything else paled into insignificance. The directors had put champagne on the coach to celebrate promotion. It remained unopened.

His assistant, Jimmy Goodfellow, was unhappy about the sparkly being on board:

> It was like we were going on a working-mens' trip. The directors had friends on the coach and there was champagne loaded on, although it remained unopened. It was as though we thought we just had to turn up and I didn't agree with it. In the other dug-out was the old Sunderland manager Bob Stokoe and he came up to me at the end and said, 'Sorry we had to spoil your party.' I said, 'It was never a party – it was still all to do!' I still feel we scored a good goal. Their 'keeper clattered 'Gwythe' as he scored from a header and I thought, 'Yes, give the goal!' The referee, though, pointed to the spot. As I ran on to treat him, I said to the ref, 'What are you doing?' and he said, 'It's a free-kick against yourselves for a foul on the 'keeper'! The ref was George Courtney. He was next in charge of the FA Cup Final. I told him later, 'You had your best and worst games in the same week!'

Dave Gwyther reminisced, 'Not that I can remember much about it – I got knocked out! Their 'keeper clattered me. They tell me I scored but it was disallowed, but I didn't know a thing about it!' Grant Davies was shattered, fearing the worst:

> Getting beat at Rochdale was a major blow and felt like the world had fallen out of my bottom! Going to Walsall for the last game had been the one that held most

fears. Len made us realise that the prize was still there, but we had to be Newport County – not flamboyant, just keep working hard – so we still had a chance.

Gary Plumley adds, 'We were saying at Xmas, "Imagine if we have to go there on the last day to go up" and lo and behold that happened, but we were full of it. It never came into our minds that we would let it slip.'

This time, the preparations were more businesslike. Goodfellow:

I said to Len, 'Let's do it as we normally do it on Saturday.' We went nice and quietly and as we came off the motorway we saw a sign saying 'Aldridge 4'. 'Ollie' said, 'That's a sign that I'm gonna score 4' and 'Gwythe' said, 'No it isn't – that's your marks out of 10 in the papers tomorrow!' I know that supporters were impressed by how many Sunderland coaches went past on their way to their game at Cardiff, but a relative of mine was on one of them and they were all talking about how many black and amber coaches they were passing!

Davies said,

It was a tremendous day. There were thousands of County fans there and I can remember seeing all the coaches and scarves hanging out of car windows on the way up – we may as well have played at home! Once we got in the dressing room, I thought, 'This is it – it's now or never.' The boys were well fired up for it.

Talisman Tynan was also confident:

Although Walsall were playing for the title, I felt that we'd go up. We deserved promotion as one of the better sides. I always remember that there was a lot of apprehension going into that game, but I just felt we could do it. There was a lot of speculation about Keith Oakes going to a big club and he was crucial to us, but we put that aside and realised we just had to concentrate on playing our natural game.

Aldridge soon settled nerves:

My highlight at Newport was that day – a great game. We were lucky to be getting a second chance and this was a much harder test, so it was important we took the game by the scruff of the neck straight away. I scored two quick goals and I couldn't see them getting back in it. My first goal was a left footer – right up into the top corner! My second probably should have been saved though!

Walsall pulled one back, but Gwyther restored the two goal lead for the interval. Davies smiled at the memory: 'I always think of Gwyther's looping header to make it 3-1 – how he got his neck to that I'll never know because he was a big lump of a lad!' Gwyther himself added, 'I was way out on the back post and just tried to head it back, although I always felt that if I could get it over their 'keeper then it had a chance of going in.' A penalty for Walsall had nerves shredded at 3-2 but then that man, to choruses of 'There's Only One Tommy Tynan', sealed it with a header to make it 4-2. County were up!

Plumley described the scenes:

> When the final whistle went we were swamped with spectators and the first one to get to me was Mike Dowler. It must have been difficult for him as, being the reserve 'keeper, we were competing for that one spot, but he jumped on my back and I've never forgotten that moment.

Neil Bailey added,

> I can remember the goals going in and you get to that point where you know you've done it. There were all sorts of emotions – relief, excitement. I vividly remember taking a corner and seeing three of my mates.

After all of the years of struggle, John Relish cruelly missed out through injury:

> It was heartbreaking for me and Dave Bruton to be injured and miss the promotion game and the Welsh Cup Final. It was an odd feeling in the stand watching it – far worse than playing – and it was hard to feel a part of it until we got back into the dressing room.

Kevin Moore will never forget the after match celebrations:

> It was like a Cup Final day. It was fantastic for us and we were so pleased for them when we won, although me and Neil Bailey were the last ones left in the bath and for about 10 minutes we felt numb after all of the emotion of it. What I will never forget is coming back on the M5. A coach was pulling alongside ours and there were all these girls hitching their skirts up and pressing their bums against the window – we were all going mad! We had a letter a few days later from them saying 'congratulations' with some photos they had taken from their coach and there's me and John Aldridge, with our

Aldridge gets County off to a sensational two-goal start at Walsall.

Gwyther makes it 3-1.

Tynan clinches it.

The 'Holy Trinity' (Tynan, Aldridge and Gwyther) celebrates.

tongues hanging out of the window! And then there were photos of them – and they were all hairy fellas in fancy dress! We met up with loads of fans back at the ground and then a couple of days later had the Welsh Cup Final to look forward to.

Aldridge gave a supporter another memory altogether:

We got stuck into the champagne and then when we got home went clubbing. I got a taxi back to me digs in Cromwell Road and a supporter came rushing over and threw his arms around me, and I threw up all over him! I was dead embarrassed but he was really pleased and said he would put it on his wall! I've often wondered if he still has it!

Tynan said,

I remember walking in to the bar for a drink after the game and immediately was given three or four bottles of champagne – mind you they didn't realise I don't like the stuff! All that sticks in my mind was that it felt like winning the FA Cup. Success breeds success and that changed everyone's perspective of the club. I vividly remember walking through town the next day and it was unbelievable! To be honest it was even better than Carl Zeiss Jena for me.

A few nights later, Shrewsbury were beaten 2-1 in the first leg of the final. It was a night marked by a continuing tribute for promotion, which, to some extent, gave it an unreal feel. Tynan scored both. Shrewsbury, however, were a formidable Second Division side and the second leg at Gay Meadow would be a stern test if a famous double was to be completed. County took them apart with goals from Tynan, Lowndes and Gwyther. Ashurst said,

Big Dave Gwyther did all the damage and was absolutely magnificent. Their Manager, Graham Turner, could not believe how they had been hammered over two legs. All of our players were coming of age.

It really was a 'Season of Triumph' with many of the players putting the success down to the close bonds formed. Oakes was regarded by all as the rock of the side and Vaughan was voted Player of the Year. Plumley further explained:

We had such a strong team and as stand out players you have to look at the

Above: Keith Oakes introduces the mayor to John Aldridge before the Welsh Cup final first leg.

Right: Tommy Tynan nets the winner but it is a slim lead to take to the second leg at Shrewsbury.

Dave Gwyther caps his man of the match display in the second leg with the final goal of the game.

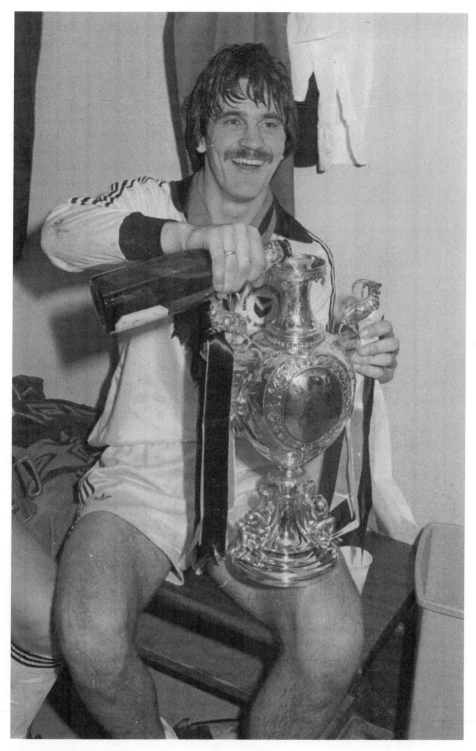

Magnificent captain Keith Oakes holds silverware at last!

guys up front who scored some tremendous goals. Tommy played just behind the forwards and he was so influential as the season drew to a close. Kevin Moore of course on the left wing was also a key player for us. Kev was so unassuming and if you didn't know you'd have never guessed from the way he was that away from the game his family were very wealthy. One day his dad brought his Rolls Royce and Kev went mad as he didn't want to be seen in it! Kev was the one though, that if he'd got the rights for diving he could have made his own fortune! He was so clever at it – but there were also times he really was clogged down and the ref said he'd dived!

The season was capped with an open-top bus ride to show off the Welsh Cup and Welsh League Championship trophy won by the reserves. Goodfellow admitted,

The celebrations on the open top bus I thought would be a nightmare – I expected us to be going past a few people waiting in bus stops waiting for their own – but it was an incredible occasion! A fella got hold of me and said, 'I never thought I would see County do this before I died!' That was very poignant and sticks with me.

Richard Walden, County's best ever right-back, joined as the first ever player sold at a transfer tribunal.

8

EUROPE TO ENFIELD

The 1980s would be a decade of the most extreme contrast. The publication of the 1980/81 season fixture list was in itself an occasion as the familiar opponents of the previous two decades were replaced by clubs who had spent much of that time at an even higher level than the Third Division. County had played at Burnley in the FA Cup when they were at polar opposite ends of the food chain, and now their next visit to Turf Moor was a League game. Next up at home were Charlton and Millwall. It felt like a very different world. Indeed, the size of ground and volume of crowd at Burnley was intimidating, although County settled and were unlucky to come away with only a point after a 1-1 draw.

The season was always though going to be about Europe. Inevitably what turned out to be one of those romantic stories that entrances supporters everywhere was not matched by League form. In fact, County's twelfth-place finish is misleading, as there was only a three-point gap from the final relegation place. County were twenty-second with only six games left and survived thanks to three wins and a draw.

The European Cup Winners' Cup began as early as 16 September, when Irish side Crusaders came to Somerton for the first leg. A Walden free-kick was headed in by Gwyther for the first ever European goal and that was followed by efforts from Moore, Aldridge and Bruton. That was a lead to relieve any pressure for their return in Belfast, but in such troubled times in Ireland, the squad's nerves were still fragile. Len Ashurst said, 'The troubles were upper-most in our minds. Some of us admittedly didn't want to go! It was a late afternoon kick-off and there was a strange atmosphere.

We toughed it out and drew 0-0.' Jimmy Goodfellow: 'At training there was an almighty bang and everyone hit the deck. There was a slate quarry behind where we were! The Irish just said "Oh, sorry!"' Gary Plumley: 'If someone trod on the ball and tripped over, we used to shout "sniper!" We said if there was one thing we wouldn't do, was that if anyone did this, we wouldn't be shouting "sniper" this time! Blow me, someone did and the whole team hit the floor!' John Relish: 'Our guide on the way to the stadium was pointing out all these places where people had been shot!' Tommy Tynan:

> On the coach, we were driven through places that were bombed out and derelict. One funny moment that broke the tension was there was an election on at the time and there was a big banner we drove past with 'Vote Tynan' on it! The hospitality, though, with what they'd been through, was second to none. Their players were waiting for us as we came out after the game to look after each of us on a one-to-one basis and they bought us Guinness and really looked after us. We found out the next day that their secretary had been robbed after the game at gunpoint!

Reserve 'keeper Mike Dowler, who had played in the first leg: 'We were on the bench just feet away from the crowd and had bad backs because we spent the whole game leaning forward as far as we could!'

Next up were Haugar ,and a 0-0 first leg was followed by a trouncing at Somerton. Relish remembers,

> I was never one to like flying and we had to go to Norway in this old two engine prop which I always remember had a picture of a ship in the cabin and they tied the door open to the cockpit to take off. I thought we would never get there! Typical County – they really splashed out!

Richard Walden:

> We were at Cardiff Airport waiting to fly out to Norway for our game against Haugar and were all quite excited. Some of the lads spotted a twin propeller green wreck that looked like something from the Second World War, which we had a joke about to pass the time away. We stopped laughing when we realised it was ours!

The Haugar groundsman welcomes Lowndes, Oakes, Davies and Vaughan to Norway.

Len Ashurst:

Our plane landed on a little island which was connected to the mainland by a bridge and we had to get a coach from there to the hotel. It was absolutely freezing and we were all a bit shocked. They had a big English centre-forward Peter Osborne and Keith Oakes had his hands full but coped with him. Actually, Oakes and Grant Davies were magnificent that game and Gary Plumley came into his own. We murdered them at home in the second leg in what I consider to be one of our best displays. You may win the odd game by fluking a goal, but you don't fluke six!

Tynan:

I scored one of the goals of which I'm most proud. It was featured in *Match Weekly* or *Shoot* and people like Bob Paisley were talking about what a good example it was of how I'd come out of the hole to play the ball out to the wing and then got back into the space to score.

Dowler: 'When we beat them 6-0 everyone on the bench was shouting, "Put me on!"'

The quarter-final draw could hardly have been less kind. Crack East German outfit Carl Zeiss Jena, laden with international stars, had already made light work of AS Roma and Valencia and were sitting two points behind their League leaders. Every County fan, even those yet to be born, could tell you that Tynan scored twice to come back with an implausible 2-2 draw and, with away goals counting double, County were in with a chance of pulling off one of the greatest shocks in the history of European competition. The game at Somerton Park was one of the greatest injustices over ninety minutes, with at least one effort from Gwyther clearly over the line and a defensive performance, including world-class saves by 'keeper Grapenthin, denying County time after time. Kurbjuweit scored a soft first-half free-kick against the run of play against a cold and fairly inactive Plumley. County were out amid tears of pride and despair, but it was Carl Zeiss who would go on to play Benfica in the semi-final and end losing finalists to Dinamo Tbilisi. Over 200 fans made the fourteen-hour trip for the first leg and 18,000 packed Somerton for the second, but below are the memories of management and staff as told to me:

Relish:

> When we were in West Germany, everything was a blaze of colour and the moment we crossed to the East everything was so grey it was like looking at an old black-and-white film. At Checkpoint Charlie it was surreal when these 'Stasi' police came on with guns and the 'Card School' with Tommy and a couple of others never missed a beat! They didn't even look up which struck me as funny at the time. Going past shops you would see queues right around the block just to get their basic necessities and even in the open fields you would see armed police!

Ashurst:

> When we got to our hotel, the streets were deserted apart from a few trams, but inside we found that their annual carnival was in full swing with a big

dance being held there. It had been a long trip but among all the noise, Jimmy Goodfellow and I turned to the players and said, 'Right lads, we won't get any sleep, so go and join the carnival, have a few drinks and join in the fun.'

Walden:

It was like day and night when you crossed the border – like being in the dark ages. It was a hell of a long bus journey and when we got there we were advised not to talk to people because of the Secret Services or to go out alone, so we mainly stuck to the hotel. On the night we got there, all fairly tired, there was a party going on and Len and Jimmy said to us to have a few beers and get to bed for 12 a.m. People were fairly surprised by that but we were sensible. The following night they put on another party to entice us in but we didn't go. I went for a walk around the market and looked at people's faces and thought, 'What's their life like?' As we walked out onto the pitch they were throwing bread rolls and things at us!

Two goals from Tommy Tynan set County up for a historic return game that left players and supporters alike drowning in tears of pride and disappointment.

Goodfellow:

There were women in fancy dress all over the hotel and we were ushered into a restaurant. We sat down and one of the lads said, 'Any chance?' I asked Len and he said, 'If you want to.' I said, 'I'm going to the bar and anyone wants to join me you can.' They thought it was a wind up! It relaxed them. The big mistake the following day was their manager watched all our training routines and we didn't know it was him! We were invited to his office though and saw all his diagrams and tactics!

Relish:

Carl Zeiss were so quick and skilful on the ball. I marked the East German international right winger. I thought when we went over that if we could get away without a real hiding we'd have done well – no one gave us a chance – but the way we played that night was fantastic – and especially so I thought was the impression our supporters made in a 'v' in the corner of the stand. How some of them got there I'll never know! There was disbelief coming off the pitch and it was a fantastic performance from Tommy and Dave Gwyther. The back four was under a lot of pressure, it was like the Alamo, but Oaksie was his usual self with a fantastically commanding performance.

Walden:

As the game went on we thought, hang on, we can match these!

Tynan:

We weren't expected to do anything except get slaughtered! At the end of the day when you look up at the score board and see 'CZJ 2 – Newport 2 (Tynan 2) – well it is of course one of the most memorable highlights of my career – and yet we were near the bottom of the League at the time! Their crowd was clapping us at the end. It was unbelievable what we did! There was a media frenzy after which for players at our club, when we weren't used to that, was also quite frightening actually! It gave us a little taste of what the big stars do.

Although Tommy grabbed the headlines with his last kick of the game equaliser, one of the most enduring images is of the part Gwyther played in the build up. Described by Ashurst as 'A piece of Gwyther magic,' Dave told me,

I was tired that's for sure! To be fair, a 2-1 defeat would have been more than respectable and being in the final minutes you would have thought a player of my experience would have just taken the ball into the corner flag. I'd picked it up on about the halfway line and was just running down the wing with it. I just kept going and could see things happening when I cut inside. It was just a spur of the moment thing. Tommy was probably screaming for it as well knowing him! Apparently Len was on the bench shouting, 'What's "Gwythe" taking it in there for?'

Dave omitted to mention that he saw off at least three Carl Zeiss defenders on his mazy run. His cross had seen a shot from Lowndes blocked and rebound to him, from where he slotted it in to Tynan to score the most famous of all County goals.

The anticipation leading up to the second leg was at fever pitch. Never had County been subject to such intense media attention and, despite the apparent gulf in class, the first-leg heroics meant that even the most sceptical quietly fancied County's chances. On any other day, County may have scored a hatful. You can't take anything away from world-class defending by the visitors, but even they would admit that clearances were in desperation rather than anticipation.

Walden:

We really believed in our chances, especially when we heard that their most capped player was being moved from left wing to 'Sweeper' which made us feel that we had them worried.

Relish:

Apart from the free-kick they scored from, I can hardly recall them having a chance and we were so dominant we ended up in the late stages playing with only two at the back! One of their defenders made an incredible clearance when he knocked it over his own bar which nine times out of ten he'd have put in his own net and we thought in the first half, one effort in particular, was over the line.

Ashurst:

We wanted to exploit them in the air and from set-pieces especially. We hit posts and bars and were seeing incredible clearances and the most exceptional defensive

Lothar Kurbjuweit and Oakes prepare for battle in the second leg.

The sixty-six-times-capped East German international breaks County hearts with the only goal to send them to the semi-final.

play from them. I have a permanent picture in my mind of Oakes' rocket-like header just before the end. I'd pushed Keith up front for the last 20 minutes. I thought that was it, we'd scored! I can remember their 'keeper's name now, Hans-Ulrich Grapenthin, and the fella pulled off the most unbelievable save. They scored from a sloppy free-kick, which went straight through Plumley's legs, although I would never blame Gary for that. We were unlucky, desperately so.

Davies:

I remember coming off the pitch crying – I was so distraught! We were prevented from winning rather than lost – the ref was rather friendly with them. We could have played until today and not scored – Gwyther's header was definitely over the line. It was an iffy free-kick for their goal but you have to give them credit for the way they defended. Keith's header at the end 99 times out of 100 would have flown into the net, but he somehow saved it. You get feelings in games that you can batter a goal and not get anything, but I always felt at Newport that we would score as we had such good players up front. It wasn't to be that night, though!

Oakes:

I can't believe to this day that my header late on was saved. From the moment it left my head I thought it was in!

Tynan:

The home game was the most nervous I've ever been. I just wish Keith's aerial prowess had for once let him down. Late on he caught it perfectly, but I was standing right behind and if he'd missed it I would have put the ball into an open net! It was an unbelievable save! When they got the goal they just shut up shop and losing that game is the biggest disappointment of my career. For weeks later I felt very deflated. Then shortly after, Len dropped me just to give me another kick up the backside again!

Gwyther:

A couple of the lads said that my header was over the line when they cleared it, but I don't know.

Goodfellow:

In a way it was good that Len and I moved on because what do you do after that? How do you top it?

Plumley:

After the game at their place when we went back, the nightclub underneath the hotel, where we thought we'd have a right old party, was almost empty – it was curfew again and there was half a dozen people and us there. We would have loved to have shared that night with supporters but we were whisked off and it felt a bit lonely and so couldn't wait to get them back to ours. I think of it as the result that never was – we annihilated them! OK, a mistake was made when I let the only goal of the game in, but I still maintain that the ball clipped Karl Elsey and changed its direction slightly, but even then I will admit that I could and should have stopped it. I took two throw-ins that night – that is how much we were attacking them! Gwyther's header was a foot over the line. Keith was heading everything – we pummelled them, but just couldn't get it past Grapenthin – or at least one that the ref would give! If it had been a boxing match it would have been stopped. It was the lowest I ever felt coming off the pitch. We swapped shirts, but it turned out that they were not allowed to give us their first team shirts, so gave us old ones that they'd used to train in!

Relish:

Looking back our priority that season was Europe and it was hard to lift ourselves for the League.

The 1980/81 season had seen the club record fee once again broken when £45,000 was paid to Spurs to bring in the immensely popular 'keeper Mark Kendall. Ineligible to play in the early rounds, it said much about Ashurst that he rewarded Plumley's loyalty against Carl Zeiss. In December, the fee was almost doubled when the man who put County into Europe, Swansea's Alan Waddle, was also signed to give more firepower; for all the wealth of striking talent County possessed, League goals were hard to come by. For 1981/82, a substantial £60,000 was also paid for Sheffield Wednesday's Player of the Year, midfielder Jeff Johnson. Both flopped spectacularly! It is unfair that all these years later County's demise is often linked to these failed signings. While to

Another Gwyther header saved by Grapenthin.

date no player's fee has come close to these, the fact remains that the money was recouped from the transfers of the likes of Tynan and Aldridge, for whom Ashurst had spent a fraction, and youth product Lowndes.

The first three games were won (the first time this had happened in forty-seven years) but from then on it was all downhill. Gates dropped by a quarter and the board, facing cutbacks, announced that assistant Goodfellow would have to go. By February, the tension was such that the previously unthinkable happened – Ashurst was sacked. How quickly things can change in the fickle, results-oriented world of football! His successor, Colin Addison, managed to lift spirits, despite having just been sacked by Derby. The 'Addo' magic eventually worked again, although there was only one win in the first fourteen games, but only two defeats in the last eleven saw relegation avoided with a 1-0 home defeat of Huddersfield in the penultimate game. The winning goal was scored by Steve Lowndes, who had set a new club record the previous season of 160 consecutive appearances. At the end of the season, Waddle left on a free transfer, with his most positive contribution remaining the penalty miss that set County up for European glory. Johnson left for just £10,000 early the following season.

There was little confidence going into 1982/83. Addison appointed a new assistant, Bobby Smith, and the main three signings to make an impression were full back Vaughan Jones (in place of the retiring Walden), the immaculate Kenny Stroud (who would replace Grant Davies, the previous season's Player of the Year but now strangely out of favour) and Welsh international Terry Boyle (who would fill in for the injured Oakes). Despite the lack of optimism, the season was to be one of the very best, with Addison's more eye-catching, expansive style of play both thrilling and getting results. The season got off to an unexpectedly brilliant start. Strong early cup form was matched with only two defeats in the opening fourteen games. First Division Everton, who were embarking on their most successful period since the 1960s, was the glamorous prize in the second round of the League Cup and a 2-0 defeat at home was improved on by a 2-2 draw in the second leg in a game County could have won. Cardiff were also vanquished in the Welsh Cup in the first of three exciting encounters as the Bluebirds were now also in the Third Division, and managed by Ashurst! Everton returned for the FA Cup third round and this time were very fortunate to take County back for a replay. Gwyther had scored for County and, with the clock ticking down, a long distance shot from out wide took Kendall by surprise. A spectacular overhead kick by Aldridge at Goodison was not quite enough as County went out 2-1.

Come February, it became apparent that County had overstretched themselves. £100,000 was needed immediately (with a debt of £300,000) and the Welsh FA, having refused to help the council, agreed to loan £120,000. The 3-0 defeat of Preston on 15 February started a run of ten wins from the next eleven games, during which even George Best, who had been linked with County, could not inspire his Bournemouth side to knock County out of their stride. The run culminated on Easter Monday with the visit of promotion rivals Cardiff. The 'Bluebirds' had won the Boxing Day encounter 3-2 with a last-minute goal. Now, in front of 16,052 fans in a closely fought encounter, County exacted revenge. In Tony Ambrosen's *Amber in the Blood*, the solitary goal of the game was credited to Relish, while the official club log says Aldridge. Relish explained to me,

> I'm pretty sure it was my goal and they did announce that, but 'Ollie' came in straight after the game and said, 'I want that goal!' and went up to the press box to tell them and they gave it to him! I don't know what I was doing up there actually, but 'Ollie' and Gary Bennett both followed it in and bundled each

other into the net, but I'm sure it was already over the line when he touched it. Thing was, 'Ollie' was battling Tommy for the 'Golden Boot' and they were really competitive with each other!

Whoever scored it, the outcome was that with just seven games to go, County were deservedly top of the League. Just three more wins were all that were needed to secure promotion. Even though the next game was lost, it was seen as a mere blip and there was a carnival atmosphere as fellow challengers Portsmouth, led again by Aizlewood, played for their destiny in front of a crowd of 10,419 (which seemed suspiciously larger). The 'Pompey Chimes' rang out loud as they scored three goals with no County reply set alarm bells ringing. Rumours were rife that County could not afford to go up and the council, having forwarded £81,000 to prevent a court appearance, appeared to give some substance to this. Wrexham were beaten 4-0, leaving three games to go, but that was simply a false dawn. A 3-0 loss in the next game was followed by a winner-takes-all event at Huddersfield. County lost 1-0 and so it was Huddersfield who celebrated. The final game was a damp squib draw 1-1 with Exeter in front of just 3,520. County had inexplicably (or not, if the conspiracy theorists were to be believed) thrown it all away. I have spoken to most of that side and to a man they have denied any pressure not to go up.

Addison:

That was arguably the biggest disappointment of my managerial career. We blew it big time! I remember calling a team meeting because someone was putting rumours about that we didn't want to go up. What a load of b******s! What went wrong? I don't know other than the pressure might have been too much.

Tynan:

Aldridge and I scored fifty-five goals that season – equalled only by Ian Rush and Kenny Dalglish. Bobby Gould said on TV that he couldn't understand how we never got promotion when we had the two best strikers in the Division. I thought we'd go up for sure after I scored a hat-trick against Wrexham with only three games to go. Addison was so upset about us not going up he cancelled our end of year function. He was absolutely gutted. There's nothing I can put my finger on to explain it. We died a death! I don't think we realised the position we were in. Why? 'Bottling it' – well, that is a bad expression for me to use, but ...

Relish 'scores' against Cardiff with Aldridge not yet even in sight.

Lowndes could not find a way through against Portsmouth and County were about to blow a Second Division return.

Kendall added:

> We were too scared of the position we were in. We were over-trained and were being given dossiers on players we were coming up against and it all became too much. They should have taken the gas off, not put the pressure on – we couldn't handle it.

One thing is for sure, as Relish summed up: 'It was the worst summer I ever had. We knew it was our fault. It was the beginning of the end, as within twelve months that side was torn apart.'

It was a depressing summer for fans, who said goodbye to Gwyther, Davies, Moore, Plumley and then, to cap it all, Tynan for a miserly £55,000 to Plymouth, where he would many years later be voted their all-time greatest player. Lowndes also left for Millwall for the same fee. In October, Vaughan and Elsey joined Ashurst's Cardiff in the Second Division with John Lewis, Linden Jones and Tarki Micallef heading the other way. They made an immediate impression, but it was Aldridge's goals that kept results favourable and his supply line was improved the day the club's first black player, Neville Chamberlain, made his debut on loan and helped him to a hat-trick in a 5-3 win over Wigan. Aldridge had scored twenty-seven goals by March and a £70,000 offer without a sell-on clause saw him leave for promotion favourites Oxford. From that point on, County were on an irreversible downward spiral and finished thirteenth and, more worryingly, without hopeful expectation of things improving. Boardroom tensions were high and George Thorneycroft resigned after a decision not to dispense with the services of Bobby Smith, who was not only an unaffordable wage but had been extremely unpopular with many of the players since his arrival.

Oakes left before 1984/85, but Addison seemed to have done well in the market, making a number of potentially strong signings, including Chamberlain and future Premiership manager Tony Pulis. Welsh international David Giles also soon signed, although he suffered the curse of the infamous No. 7 shirt and became the target of terrace impatience. The most important transfer would in years to come be seen as an even costlier poor decision than the Waddle purchase: the sale of the ground back to the council. County finished eighteenth in an uninspiring season, which should have been memorable for two cup exploits. Firstly, in the Welsh Cup, a semi-final with non-league Bangor should have been a passport to Europe as Shrewsbury once again defeated Swansea in the other tie. Losing 1-0 at Bangor was shocking; drawing

0-0 at Somerton in a performance totally devoid of belief was unforgivable! Just as bad was that, having fortuitously reached the Southern Area Final of the Freight Rover Trophy away to Brentford, they lost 6-0, and with it an appearance at Wembley. At the end of May, Addison resigned so the club could survive and a few days later Smith, who many felt should already have left, stepped up. Secretary Phil Dauncey was made redundant, so Keith Saunders, who had spent a lifetime at Somerton and was rewarded with a testimonial in 1978, returned part time. There were only twelve professionals on the books when the campaign started, one of whom was the celebrated Welsh international Leighton James, who had come in as player-coach. Predictably, results were poor and the financial clouds hung heavy. However, if the ground sale had been short-sighted, the initiative to set up a Lifeline Society, launched by legendary England international Nat Lofthouse, was inspired and had raised £40,000 by the end of the season; in a few years, its presence would be even more significant. With relegation looking likely, Smith resigned and the injured Relish agreed to take on the management role. His impact would have made Addison proud, with players clearly stepping up a gear for a man they all respected. James' contacts were also useful and ex-England star Bob Latchford, at one time the most expensive player in the country, added his class and experience to the cause. The last two games were crucial to avoid the drop and an injury time winner from Jones at Gillingham meant just one point was needed at Blackpool in the last game. That was secured with a 0-0 draw, finishing nineteenth.

County had escaped, but not for long. Relish didn't want the post and Jimmy Mullen took over as player-manager. The disillusioned James left, as did Pulis and Boyle. The club was in tatters. The League Cup summed up the difference that just a few years had made. Instead of pushing Everton, the aggregate score was 1-9. County finished rock-bottom and headed back to the Fourth Division. The season had been punctuated by on and off reports of Canadian businessman Jerry Sherman making a £750,000 takeover bid. Having had his offer accepted, he had demanded the board resign and then disappeared. Boardroom changes did not prevent the club going into administration in February, prompting Sherman out of his hiding hole. Mullen had enough and left, leaving senior pro John Lewis to add management to his CV. There was emerging talent in the side but there was no time to nurture it. County had to cash in, and eighteen-year-old 'keeper Roger Freestone, who had stepped up after Kendall's £25,000 sale to Wolves, was quickly moved on for a record fee to Chelsea, potentially rising to £160,000. Despite this, County made it to the Welsh Cup final. Merthyr were

Right: John Aldridge made a quick
return with Oxford, seen here
pre-match with Terry Boyle.

Below: How County could have done
with his goals against Bangor in the
Welsh Cup semi-final.

Two England centre-forwards lent their support to the County cause – Nat Lotfhouse with Bobby Smith at the Lifeline Society launch.

Bob Latchford, who gave everyone a lift.

a much harder proposition than Bangor should have been, and proved to be a real challenge as County were kicked off the park in a replay after the first game was drawn 2-2 with Latchford (now with the Martyrs) undoing his previous favour by scoring. County had again missed out on a European adventure that may have been a lifeline. John Lewis told me,

When Sherman came on the scene everyone was thinking 'here is our knight in shining armour', but I'm always suspicious if they are talking about putting in money and certainly – with no disrespect – why Newport County? Me and Dai Williams met him in London with Maurice Salway. He said to us, 'How much do you want – £30,000, £40,000, £50,000?' I told him, 'for £17,500 we can sign Jimmy Gilligan.' He'd been on loan and he would have come, but we didn't have the money. He didn't let us have it of course and after that I knew he was a chancer. He wasn't a director so why should he pump money in? What was his angle? There was nothing to asset strip! I was naïve and young, but the things I had to do! I had to put out the 'Retained List' before the final! We thought the

John Lewis
playing against
Wrexham in
the Welsh Cup
semi-final.

game was going to be played to a conclusion and not a replay and a lot of the boys had booked their holidays! It was one of the lowest points of my career and when you think we beat Shrewsbury and Wrexham to get there. We were paired against Merthyr and despite the league they were playing in they probably had more experience in their side!

Worse was to come. The stay in the Fourth Division was not to be a long one this time – County slipped straight out and into non-league, there no longer even being a re-election campaign to contest, with automatic relegation for the bottom club to the Conference. On 16 June, the *Argus* had headlined 'The End of the Road' with £400,000 being understood as needed to survive; on the 22nd, it was confirmed that £160,000 was needed within a few days. By early August, creditors had accepted a rescue package. Linden Jones, who had provided wholehearted service since that Cardiff swap-shop, had left for Reading for £33,000 and it was agreed to accept £30,000 from Chelsea to settle the Freestone transfer. Eyebrows were raised when another eighteen-year-old local boy, Richard Jones, was subject of an £85,000 bid from Wimbledon, but this fell through. County's future was so fragile it was decided they would not even feature on Pool's coupons. Lewis, who was facing an impossible task, was sacked and, perversely for all the troubles, some of the biggest names in the game, such as Bobby Moore and Lawrie McMenemy, were being touted to replace him.

I vividly remember desperately hanging off the corner of the bed on one leg trying to get reception for BBC Wales for the long-awaited announcement to be made. They trailed it teasingly throughout and hundreds of young and older fans were searching draws for autograph books ready to meet the legend who would save the day. 'Who the **** is Eastick?' rang out from supporters who no longer knew whether to laugh or cry, as former Palace reserve 'keeper Brian Eastick, who had coached clubs at youth level, was unveiled. At least five days later, County came out of administration. Local builder Brian Stent became chairman and made money available for transfers, including the £15,000 purchase of one-time apprentice and future Welsh international Paul Bodin. The loan market was also heavily relied upon. However, for one reason or another, by season's end forty-one players had worn the shirt, with all too many being undeserving, sometimes through attitude as much as calibre. Much of the board resigned in February, followed by Stent. In early March, Eastick was ordered to do a fire sale and Bodin, who had barely had time to resettle into his surrounds, was on his way again for a tidy profit. Eastick was not far behind

Darren Peacock, seen here challenging Wolves' England cap Steve Bull, went on to Premiership fame with Kevin Keegan's Newcastle after County folded.

A fittingly gloomy photograph taken before the last League game v. Rochdale.

them; upon being sacked, he commented that should County now go through, there should be questions asked such was the scale of work he had done on reducing the wage bill and through sales. There was a setback when the council exercised prudence with the £60,000 they had offered and held this back.

David Williams stepped up into the manager's job, completing the full set for the man who can make perhaps make a greater claim than anyone to the title 'Mr Newport County'. A boyhood fan, apprentice, and first teamer with 355 appearances, Williams had fulfilled just about every backroom role since retiring (apart from secretary) and indeed later became one of the founding directors of the reformed club. He told me,

I loved being manager – I had always dreamt about doing that – but the timing wasn't very good! In the games we had left to play, about six of our ten YTS boys made their debuts. Norman Parselle was the one who stood out. Lee Sharp was also only sixteen when he played against us that season for Torquay, but he murdered us and went after that to play for Manchester United. The only good thing about that period was beating Darlington away and Swansea went up. We played Wolves at home in one of our last games in front of a good crowd, which was a good experience for the kids. The whole thing came too early for them though – or too late whichever way you look at it! The board never involved me – I just got on with the football. I just had to try and keep the players together. Going out of the League was dreadful – a sad, sad day!

Against Peterborough, an unwanted club record was set for the lowest League gate – 988. The last League away game at Darlington gave some momentary celebration, winning 2-0, but the final sombre match, with relegation already assured, was lost 1-0. Only 2,560 could face it and eight teenagers in the side did well to keep the score down. Many fans say, 'I have seen it all!' but for Supporters' Club president Bill Limbrick it was true, as he had attended County's very first game at Risca in 1912. How can you begin to describe the emotion he felt when the referee's whistle blew full time on League football at Somerton? He said,

It's a sad day, but we've known this was going to happen for a long time. You can't blame these lads, they do their best and I don't even blame the present board, because the problems started years ago with bad managers and silly transfer deals.

Before the game, Bill pointed to the crowd and said, 'Listen to that, where have they been all season? It makes me feel bitter that they come today when the support doesn't mean anything and can't help us at all.' Club Secretary Keith Saunders added, 'I just can't believe it.'

Williams resigned his management responsibility, the directors, the Worthy brothers, stood down and Supporters' Club representative Maurice Salway announced a consortium from London. They appointed Eddie May and well-known Welsh international John Mahoney as his assistant. With this new interest could there one day be a way back? If so, it would not be easy, as the council evicted the club from Somerton over an owed £23,000. May was into his post for less than a month when he thought better of it and resigned, becoming the club's only unbeaten manager, not having played a game. Mahoney took charge, and amid non-payment of wages, he somehow reached the season's starting line with the council being paid up just twenty-four hours before the big kick-off. The first Conference game saw a 3-0 defeat at Stafford. Non-league was a higher standard than many had realised and County were in the early days outclassed and outfought. Against Barnet, two players from

Gwent County side Albion Rovers were used. County lost 7-1. Bit by bit, though, Mahoney was making signings who would provide some rich entertainment, such as gazelle-like Paul Sanderson and the sublimely skilful Paul Sugrue. Their performances were not yet matched by results, but they gave some hope. That enigmatic Canadian Jerry Sherman was back on the scene and making promises galore. The problem was that the cheque was constantly in the post. This would become a recurring statement and investigative journalism alleged past fraud on his part. On 31 October, a petition to have the club wound up was presented to court, but County meanwhile were staying in top hotels and eating in top restaurants. In November, it was confirmed that Sherman was not chairman and a large sponsorship deal announced with his company, JLA Atlantic, whose logo replaced the *Argus* on shirts. On 17 February, Sherman claimed he had at last ordered that all debts be cleared, having claimed he had deposited the money, and the go-ahead was given for new signings. Mahoney had already brought in some experienced players, including Roger Gibbins, who had been a consummate pro in his first spell at the club, and classy striker Ian Thompson. Although rooted at the bottom, there was enough in this side to stage a revival and stay up and even make a challenge next season. County just seemed a 'keeper away from a decent side and the veteran Kenny Allen was persuaded to dust off his gloves and give up his day job. The bailiffs, however, had been in and taken equipment. On 23 February, Kidderminster came to Somerton for a Clubcall Cup game. Only 895 were there to see an incredible goal fest with the class of Thompson (2), Sugrue (2) and Sanderson astonishingly being outscored by the visitors (6). Allen had not been available but even rusty would have made a difference. The tiny crowd cheered them off, disappointed but fully entertained, and oblivious to the fact that would be the last time they would see their heroes.

On 27 February, a winding-up order was issued and on 1 March the club were told to appear in court and pay up or fold. The next day was officially the end. It need not have been even then, and 300 Lifeline members voted to continue the society with £50 donated to every (now unemployed) staff member. The ground was symbolically padlocked on 19 March. The League met to discuss the crisis and Enfield were required the next day to travel to Newport to go through the formality of the referee calling it off at 3.01 p.m. Somerton was a sad sight, going from full in Europe to empty against Enfield in just eight years! A two-week appeal was allowed against expulsion and, with five minutes to spare, Sherman did just that. On April Fools' Day, the club's belongings were auctioned with the media, predictably homing in on the black arm bands. Only £12,000 was raised. A week later, the League, with County's credibility shot, disallowed the appeal and on 4 April the results were expunged. Even in May, Sherman was appealing! Sanderson had scored the last ever goal and he told me,

I signed initially on a non-contract basis and later they gave me a contract, which turned out to be the worst thing I did as then the cheques started bouncing! Training was well organised and even off the field, on the face of it, things seemed quite good. Within a month or so, though, rumours started going around. Jerry Sherman would be saying one week that the money he was putting into the club was going to be paid in Deutschmarks and the next week it was going to be in Yen, but the money was never moved over as he was promising.

Sugrue added,

For a while we felt like a First Division club with overnight stays in hotels and doing things properly. If anyone could spend anyone else's money Sherman could!

David Williams surely filled more roles than anyone else in football!

The squad line-up for a short life in the Conference but few were still there at the death.

It didn't last though and we didn't get paid for six or seven weeks and knew that Mahoney was putting his hand in his own pocket. He and Les Chappell were great. It was heartbreaking to go through the club folding, especially for the fans.

Meanwhile supporters were facing reality, with just a few who had hopelessly aligned themselves with the Walter Mitty-like Sherman still believing in miracles. On 14 April, over 400 at a special general meeting of the Lifeline Society considered the possibility of starting a new club.

9

FOOTBALL WITH A FUTURE

It is hard to describe the sense of loss when you lose your club. Many supporters have at times struggled with the anxiety of the prospect, but it actually happening? Relatively few experience this, and at the time County folded it was even more uncommon – somehow a solution always seemed to arrive. County had played Bristol City immediately after they reformed as a new company part way through the 1981/82 season and simply continued, but that was no longer permissible. When taking Europe by storm, everyone wanted to be associated with the club, but few were anywhere to be seen now. Thankfully, there were those among the County faithful who simply would not lay the club to rest. Newport AFC rose like a phoenix from the ashes and, while not being the same legal entity, embodied the spirit of County. David Hando, whose leadership as chairman became synonymous with the reformed club, talked to me about this historic event:

We set up a steering committee of Lifeline and Supporters' Club members and agreed to set up a new club with the aim of restoring League football to the town. The committee of fifteen was each allocated roles and Mark Williams, the secretary, contacted the Hellenic League while I was dealing with the council – I would rather have swapped! Sherman's promises were still continuing and we did say that we would offer our full support if the original club survived. The critical date was 1 April as that was the auction, but our so-called saviours let it all go for a measly few thousand. We said to Sherman if we were offered a place in a lower league by the deadline then we would take it and he ridiculed us. The council said that we were 'Newport County in disguise' and were trying to get back into Somerton Park while we owed them money and the FAW said we were nothing to do with Newport County and had to start off in the Newport and District League! They couldn't both be right! Meanwhile a few clubs opposed us at first joining the Hellenic League – well, not so much joining, but that they thought we should join below their Premier Division. We did a rather fine prospectus to circulate – and let's face it, County had been rather good at that in the old days when fighting for re-election year after year! Everyone was very impressed with it and we then rang round, but said we had a problem as the FAW would not sanction us to play in an English league and the council would not let us play at Somerton Park, or even Glebelands, which was being talked about. One or two clubs considered a ground share, but they had reserve sides and the only one that didn't was Moreton. It was 85 miles away! I went with Ray Taylor to see their ground and can remember saying, 'Well, it's not exactly Wembley, but it's a good start!' Turning up at Moreton for our first game against Pegasus was emotional, particularly as they had repainted the railing behind the goalposts black and amber. They did everything they could to make us feel at home. 18 June saw over 400 cram into Lysaghts on a sweltering evening for the launch of Newport AFC. They cheered the launch of the club; they cheered the introduction of John Relish as manager; they cheered the signing of Graham Rogers, Barrie Vassallo, Gary Spink and Robert Painter; they cheered the amber and black strip; they cheered our friends from Moreton; they cheered the Transporter Bridge logo; they cheered the Steering Committee and voted them directors of Newport AFC Ltd and they bought £15,000 worth of shares on the night; and they cheered our slogan 'Football with a Future.' I warned them not to believe rumours that Moreton-in-Marsh was 75 miles away, saying 'In fact it's 85!' They even cheered that! All our plans were proceeding but we had these two great disappointments with the FAW and the council. Alan Evans at the FAW was personally very supportive initially and he bought £100 worth of shares, but he had a phone call and when he came back in he'd changed. I am sure that if we'd immediately assumed the identity of the old club and Somerton Park was our home it would have been ok, but there was another problem for the FAW in that Barry Town also wanted to go in the Hellenic League and that posed them a huge problem. As it was, they reformed as Barri and went into the Beazer Midland Division, one above us, as a place became available. It was the League of Wales proposal that changed Evans – I'm sure it was not his decision and he had to eat his words and be the driving force for it. We were all making suggestions for a manager and I think that Martin

Greenham rang John Relish for advice and he got interested and said, 'What about me?' There could have been no better choice.

Relish added, 'We made a conscious effort to connect the club with local lads and these gave us an identity.' In a side containing experienced players like Barrie Vassallo, assistant manager Graham Rogers and Brian Preece, Relish made a surprising choice of captain, although all could soon see why, in Norman Parselle, a survivor of the Rochdale game and still in his teens!

Parselle told me,

I was well shocked to be asked to be captain and asked why. He said that he could have gone for an easy option, but believed that the role should also bring something extra out of the captain and thought it would do that for me, even though I was only nineteen. I was surprised by how many turned out for our first ever pre-season friendly at Kidlington. Our supporters went everywhere in numbers and without doubt they added something to your game. When we travelled it was like family outings and we were able to get really close to the supporters.

Another former County player, Chris Lilygreen, scored the first ever AFC goal in that game, which finished 4-0. He told me, 'The only thing in my head that day was that I wanted to score the first goal and I did when I was put through and scored from the right-hand side. I got a second later from a flick on the near post.'

A crowd of 594 made their way to Moreton-in-Marsh for the first League game against Pegasus Juniors and it was Parselle who scored the only goal

Graham Rogers assisted Relo in setting up AFC and set a League record as manager of the Champions in 1994/95.

in front of Sky News cameras, with the loyal defiance of supporters now attracting national attention. Parselle recalled,

> Do you know that I worked my first ever night shifts as a postman that week and I was all over the shop! They were good as gold though and let me come home early as they knew I had an important game. I went to bed at five and probably got to sleep at six and was up again at nine ready for a fair old trek to the Cotswolds. I slept on the back of the bus. I scored as well!

Despite this, Sherman was still calling himself chairman of Newport County and his 'club' was accepted into the Vauxhall Opel League. Mahoney actually took a training session at Tredegar Park the day after the Kidlington game, but on 14 August, they were kicked out of that League, again failing to fulfil obligations. In September, the decision was made to pay £8,000 to buy the name of Newport County and with that Sherman faded away, not to be heard

John Relish, one of the most influential stars in the club's history.

of again until 2005, when he was indicted and in 2007 given a seven-year prison sentence for swindling investors out of more than $1 million to fund a youth hockey team. In October, fans for once did not need a map to get to the game as Cardiff were drawn away in the Welsh Cup. Relish told me: 'One of my proudest achievements was taking them to Ninian Park. There was a superb turnout from Newport and we performed so well, losing only 1-0. I can't tell you how proud I was of them that night.'

The signings of former County Youth players David Jarvis, who scored twenty-two in twenty-five games, and Dean Herritty, whose father and uncle had starred for the club, completed the hastily assembled squad and the championship was won on a memorable night at promotion rivals Abingdon in the penultimate game, with two goals from Lilygreen and one from Jarvis taking the points in a 3-1 win. County had the chance to complete a memorable 'double' as they were to play Abingdon again in the League Cup final. A superb drive from outside the area by Herritty was cancelled out, and the Oxfordshire side objected to the replay being at Moreton. The game was therefore held over until the beginning of the following season, but glory was merely delayed, with Robbie Painter scoring the only goal of the game. Lilygreen, who finished top scorer with twenty-eight, said,

> The game at Abingdon was brilliant. I got two, a diving header and one like at Kidlington. I should have had a hat-trick but hit the bar. I felt the night was ours even though they had a good side – I never had any doubts. Great celebrations, but me and Chris Stanton were on nights and went to work when we got back at three in the morning after a meal at Lahore!

The pressure on the council and the FAW from the constant media coverage was telling; they relented and County returned to a now derelict Somerton Park. Hando said,

> It had been systematically thieved and every bit of copper pipe was stolen and it was just as well that in Graham Rogers we had a plumber amongst us! We spent £21,000 to get up to scratch. So many people worked so hard on it and everyone said it looked better than it had done for years!

The first game was a friendly against Moreton in front of 2,534 and a new league record of 2,271 was set against Redditch, but it was an anticlimax, losing 1-0. In fact, the pressure of playing at the spiritual home was hard to handle while lifting visitors, but the arrival of ex-County player Phil Green saw an upturn in form ending in an encouraging seventh.

During the season, there was some unsettling talk about the Welsh FA's idea of creating a League of Wales, while more positively, discussions were continuing with the council about a new stadium at Spytty Park. The 1991/92 season enjoyed a good start, but the Welsh FA placed increasing pressure on their members playing in the English Pyramid to join the League of Wales. For AFC, it was not an option, with the glamour of occasional European competition as the prize being a poor substitute for the mission to return to the Football League. The affected clubs banded together as the 'Irate 8', but when the FA decided to impose membership and ban them from playing in England, the resolve of some broke down.

A tribunal heard an appeal but that, aside from Merthyr's claim, was lost and the decision was taken to once more head into exile – this time a ground share with Gloucester City. Results had dropped off but recovered to again finish seventh, and the final game at Somerton Park saw Jason Prew score the only goal on what was a sad occasion. The stand on the Paddy's Bar side of the ground had also recently been destroyed by fire. Welsh FA president Tommy Forse infamously stated that AFC was 'No more Welsh than Gateshead', while secretary Evans added that the Welsh exiles would go bust within two years and that the three Football League clubs would be part-time within four! County were to embark on a long and costly legal challenge. Hando told me,

The second time in exile, it was very wearing and it put us £200,000 in debt. If we'd lost our High Court case we'd have all been bankrupt. We picked up on the optimism of our solicitor, Charlie Hopkins, who was convinced we would win. The FAW didn't think we'd have the will or the money to take them to court. You could tell in both the interim and full cases that the judges seemed to be sympathetic to the points we made. Before that there had been an FAW tribunal with Vernon Pugh QC, which they claimed was independent, but he would not let us argue restraint of trade. His judgment was in favour of Merthyr and against the other seven of what had become known as the 'Irate 8' of Welsh clubs fighting for the right to play in the English pyramid system. He said that Merthyr, being in the Conference, were nearer to the League, to which I answered, 'You have argued our case which is all about progression!'

Some famous names lined up at Gloucester with Mark Kendall, Linden Jones and Steve Lowndes calling time on their League careers and later being joined by John Lewis and Nigel Vaughan. Their legs may no longer have moved so swiftly but their class was still apparent and at one stage good progress was being made in four cup competitions. This was at the expense of League prospects as, with a fixtures backlog and injuries mounting, form dipped. The tension of the situation mounting, Relish resigned. He told me,

> I resigned after we had lost at home to Rushden. I'd been at a meeting in Manchester that day and didn't get there until just before half-time. The travelling was really taking its toll and I felt that we were looking tired and needed either a new team or a new manager. I probably made a mistake.

Rogers stepped up and steered the side to a fifth-place finish. On 2 June, a Past v. Present game was played at Somerton Park prior to its being demolished for housing, with many famous names from County's glorious and not so glorious (but affectionately remembered) years taking part. Rogers told me, 'I scored the last goal in a 4-4 draw. Keith Cooper was the ref and said, "That'll do lads – that's the end of an era!"' One guest was Darren Peacock, who had stayed until County's death and now, too late for County to profit, was a Premiership star.

The following season (1993/94) saw crowds drop alarmingly to between 200 and 300, with seventy-nine diehards watching the Dr Martens Cup game with Stourbridge. Rogers was adding to the side astutely and had they been in their stride earlier they could have enjoyed a remarkable promotion against all odds, with thirteen of the final fourteen won. There was some silverware to celebrate, beating their landlords 1-0 to win the Gloucestershire Senior Cup. Forest Green were beaten 8-3 away, but the most outstanding victory was in July in the High Court. County, along with Caernarfon and Colwyn Bay, won an injunction to allow a temporary return – in County's case, to the council's newly built stadium at Spytty. Hando added,

> We were involved in the design of Spytty, although I put my foot down at one stage about the requirements of the Harriers, who were to move from Glebelands, and said we'd have to look elsewhere. I wasn't worried about the track because, let's face it, we were used to that at Somerton – I wasn't so happy about the hammers landing on the pitch! People said, 'Don't worry, when you are ready for the League the ground will be too', and the council's letter helped

in court when Evans argued that we didn't even have a ground that would be eligible.

The opening game at Spytty again featured Redditch and 2,475 were thrilled after the players emerged to the sound of Thin Lizzy's 'The Boys Are Back in Town' by a 4-0 win, the first goal at the new home being scored by Mark Tucker after just six minutes.

Rogers had introduced a vital ingredient – ex-County youngster Ceri Williams from Merthyr, who surprisingly was partnered up front by Linden Jones, who had played over 400 games in the Football League at full back. By the end of the season, they had scored fifty-seven between them. More importantly, County finished with a goal difference of +67, scoring 106 and winning the League by a margin of fourteen points. That included a record fourteen consecutive wins. At one stage, twenty points clear, the promotion-winning game at Dudley with four games remaining lacked the euphoria of previous promotions as it was clinched when back in the dressing room, when other results came through and had long been a foregone conclusion. The championship was clinched in style with another 4-0 win against Rothwell. That would take some topping, but it would have been for nothing had the success not been matched in court. Just before the first appearance, there had been an unusual incident against King's Lynn. The referee could not continue after the break and AFC fourth official Peter Blay came down from the press box to act as linesman. Midway through the half, the stand-in ref suffered the same fate. Secretary Mike Everett was qualified and he was allowed to step onto the line as well, much to the credit of the visitors, who could have understandably objected to a director judging offsides.

Meanwhile, a FIFA official was trying to find a resolution and was asking that litigation be deferred for him to take it to a UEFA meeting in Moscow, but the FAW refused. The case was heard and there was an agonising two-week wait for the judge's verdict. Court 56 was packed with supporters as Mr Justice Blackburne gave the news everyone outside of the FAW prayed for. In July, AFC returned once more to hear the court order the FAW to lift their block on rejoining the Gwent FA – Newport were home to stay!

Now just one rung below the Conference, expectations were high, but the squad were not getting any younger and at this level each step up was a noticeable difference. The first five games were won, but then just three in the next sixteen and they finished a reality-jolting fourteenth. Rogers, suffering some ungrateful abuse from the terraces, had decided he had taken them as far as he could and resigned. Nigel Vaughan took over with Will Foley as his assistant, but the board were unhappy with their terms and decided for the first time to interview and appoint former Aston Villa star Chris Price. Vaughan regretted not getting the post; the board regretted it even more as they came to terms with relegation. Price exited and in came Tim Harris, a former reserve 'keeper, who had managed Cinderford and established a good reputation. A poor run-in saw a seventh-placed finish, but that was encouraging and the foundations of a decent side were laid.

By January 1999, the debts accumulated in exile were at a critical stage. A new board took over with John Williams at the helm and put in place a rescue plan. A poll resulted in the full name 'Newport County AFC' being adopted for the following season, and to ensure that this famous name was proudly displayed twenty years after the 'Season of Triumph', promotion was fittingly won. Karl Bayliss had made a big impression in his first season and followed this up with thirty-one goals. Eleven of the final sixteen games were won, with ex-Cardiff star Carl Dale making his quality count, and the runners-up spot was clinched by beating Solihull 4-1 with two games remaining. What a wonderful way to finish a decade as AFC! The classic 'Terra Marique' crest was restored on shirts for 1999/2000 and a fabulous start to the season made the prospects of a Conference return more than a pipe dream. This was not sustained in the second half of the campaign, but finishing seventh was very commendable with County looking more than comfortable, roared on by new Mascot 'Spytty the Dog'. The new millennium, with Dale now enjoying a fruitful partnership up front with Garry Shephard, saw an eventful game at Cambridge City. After thirty-five minutes, County were trailing 4-0. A consolation was scored before half-time but in the second half there was a glimmer of hope when a second was netted. Cambridge extended their lead to 5-2, surely killing the game, but Shephard had other ideas, his hat-trick bringing off a sensational 6-5 win. Nevertheless, given the previous season, a tenth-place finish was a bit of a let down. There was almost some glory in the Dr Martens Cup, but the semi-final was lost at Worcester 5-3. Williams had resigned as chairman in January 2001 and was replaced by founding director Wallace Brown, who initially shared the role with Martin Greenham. The early efforts to turn around finances were reversing and Brown's tenure was concerned with 'keeping the wolf from the door.' However, cup glory was the story of the 2001/02 season, when County reached the first round of the FA Cup for the first time since reformation. Blackpool away was almost a famous giant-killing, but leading 2-1, a late penalty was conceded. A ground record 3,721 attended the replay and could not contain their excitement when Matt Rose put County ahead. The game went to extra time when full-time training made the difference, and Blackpool eased through with a flattering 4-1 scoreline. Harris was building a formidable side of experience and youth and finished in their highest position yet – fifth. You had to wonder if the twenty-two cup games had cost a serious promotion challenge. One of these had been Swansea in the FAW Premier Cup third round, featuring live on TV for the second time that season. The Swans won 3-0. The Gwent Senior Cup was won for the second time in three seasons. Season 2002/03 saw a League club beaten for the first time, but also saw the resignation of Harris. An initial strong start quickly nosedived and a humiliating defeat in the FA Cup to the students of Team Bath saw Newport-born seventy-three-times-capped Welsh international Peter Nicholas assume command in November. There was no great improvement and County finished tenth. However, Swansea returned in the FAW Premier Cup and this time their feathers were ruffled as County gave them a lesson, winning 3-1. Up next was Cardiff in the semi-final. It was 0-0 after extra time and Spytty was fevered when Richard French's effort won the penalty shoot-out. To win the trophy it would have to be done the hard way, with a visit to the remaining Welsh League club Wrexham in the final. The Robins were free-scoring and enjoying a promotion year with the likes of Lee Trundle in their ranks; as bravely as County battled, the gulf in class was all too obvious and the game was lost 6-1. During the season, Paddy Mullen had called a meeting of local businessmen, knowing that another crisis was in prospect. A shadow board was established to put the club on a better footing. Gradually the shadow team took over, with Chris Blight later becoming chairman.

2003/04 was a particularly important season as the teams finishing in the top half would qualify for the newly proposed Conference (South). Failure effectively meant relegation, with another rung being added to the tier. And that looked precisely the outcome with a woeful start. Inconsistency followed but a win at Dorchester and a superb 2-1 victory at champions Crawley saw County secure their place in seventh, just four points to the good. The FAW Premier Cup again saw a visit by Cardiff, but this time County lost 1-0. At least the Gwent Cup stayed on the mantelpiece! Among players joining for

2004/05 was Welsh international Jason Bowen, who proved to be an excellent signing. It was not long though before Nicholas was sacked and another Welsh cap, John Cornforth, appointed. He failed to make any impression, and at eighteenth, County now had the feeling of simply treading water. Who cared that the Gwent Cup was won again?

2005/06 was more of the same, with an identical eighteenth-place finish, only this time it would be known as 'The Great Escape II'. Cornforth was replaced as early as September, with Academy coach and former 'keeper Glyn Jones stepping in as caretaker until Peter Beadle was appointed. His signing of 'keeper Tony Pennock was hugely important and he would be affectionately called 'The Master'. New striker Craig Hughes, more commonly known as Guppy, would also become a cult hero. However, with just ten games left, County were ten points adrift. The leadership skills of centre back John Brough were added and a revival Addison would have been proud of was on its way. The penultimate game at Cambridge City secured safety in a quite remarkable turnaround. County lost their grip on the Gwent Cup – kicked out for not fulfilling a tie!

Beadle built on this for 2006/07, bringing in League experience with Julian Alsop, Damon Searle and Steve Jenkins. Everyone was distressed by a serious pre-season injury to Pennock, but he was ably replaced by Mark Ovendale. The football was at times dazzling, and some high-scoring games lit up the results table, including a 4-0 win at Dorchester, even being topped by a goal in the next game against champions-elect Histon. Unfortunately, a fixture backlog meant nine matches in twenty-one days, and this ultimately told, but they came so close to the play-offs! The penultimate game at Weston-super-Mare saw a 3-0 half-time lead pulled level, but Sam O'Sullivan scored the winner 2 minutes into added time! That had depleted the final dregs of energy and the comparatively easy offering of Cambridge City at Spytty was a game too many and was lost 2-1. The backlog was the result of challenging on three Cup fronts. In the FA Cup, the first round proper was reached for only the second time – and a glamour tie it was too – Swansea at home! The team had been filmed listening to the draw, with Cardiff die-hard Guppy going ballistic with excitement. The game is regrettably remembered as a bad-tempered affair in front of a record 4,616 crowd, one of whom ensured the club made headlines for the worst possible reasons by throwing a coin that hit the linesman, forcing his departure. County lost 3-1. Wrexham were beaten en route to the FAW Premier final against TNS at Spytty, but this was also an anticlimax, losing 1-0. Guppy disagreed that this was down to fatigue: 'It wasn't the fatigue that did us – it was the pressure. You could sense the pressure getting to us – you'd read the *Argus* and you'd spend all your time thinking you had to do it – and then we let ourselves and everybody down.'

Beadle told me,

> To be honest, doing so well in the cups brought the money in, but it meant our League form suffered as we had so many games to catch up with and it took its toll. We believed we could get in the play-offs and on the last day I felt both pride for how far we'd come so quick, but of course disappointment for the supporters who'd travelled in numbers far and wide and for the board who had backed me too. We reached the final of the FAW Premier Cup and it was a bit surreal playing New Saints on our own pitch, but we didn't do ourselves justice and were lucky to finish with just a 1-0 defeat. Perhaps it was the beginning of the end, as the minimum expectation the next season was the play-offs.

The 2007/08 season was dramatic, but unexpectedly Beadle's last. Inconsistency in the League was frustrating, but just four points were needed from the last three games to reach the play-offs. The first was secured against Eastbourne, leaving just one win needed from the final two home games. These were miserably lost 4-1 against Thurrock and 2-1 to Fisher, and instead County finished ninth. The FAW Premier Trophy, however, was won. Beadle told me:

> We beat both Swansea and Cardiff in the FAW Premier Cup and that was unbelievable. Cardiff away was particularly special as they'd started the game with such a strong side. We got to 90 minutes and I was really concerned about us hanging on but the lads stepped up to the plate and it was 1-1 after extra time. Damon Searle was unlucky with his penalty that hit the crossbar, but they missed theirs, Lee Jarman scored and Glyn Thompson saved for us! We were ecstatic when we won. We again, though, lost out on the play-offs by losing the last game. That Fisher game was extremely close. A few games we should have won, but all managers can say that, but for Fisher I think the pressure maybe got to a few – we certainly didn't prepare any differently. We finished ninth, which doesn't look great, but it was so close. I was sacked the next day!

Guppy recalled,

> We beat the Jacks with a last-minute goal from Charlie Griffin but when he

scored I didn't go to him – I went straight to their fans! I enjoyed that. In the final against Llanelli, I got the winner 8 minutes from time. The ball came to me almost on the goal line right next to Andrew Legg and I beat him to it and ran off doing the 'show me the money' actions. We had a bonus and were going to Marbella. The club got a lot of money for winning the Cup.

2008/09 was a season of transition under new manager, ex-Premiership star Dean Holdsworth, who had enjoyed a spell at County in 2006/07. Most of the experienced names left, with Jason Bowen a particular loss, and there was a revolving door of new faces, some who departed just as quickly, but slowly names would arrive who would write themselves in County history, including Craig Reid, Sam Foley and future Premier League and England international Danny Rose. County pulled themselves from the lower reaches of the table to finish tenth. There is something about the end of a decade that County simply love, though, and 2009/10 was to be a record-breaking campaign. Captained by new signing Gary Warren, County were top by September and promoted in front of 4,221 in mid-March against Havant and Waterlooville, thanks to two Sam Foley goals.

By the season's end, County had finished with 103 points, twenty-eight clear of second-placed Dover. Holdsworth told me,

I realised what we could do the day we beat Eastleigh 5-1 at home and after the game I went in the dressing room and said, 'We will win this League – so get ready!' And that was in early September! I think that season we were the first team in Europe to get promotion. The euphoria – seeing grown men crying – I'll never forget the feeling. I had to control the team as I wanted them to just not win it but make themselves heroes and put their names in the history of the club. I think there were about eight records we broke that year! The players deserve huge credit for sustaining their professionalism as we could so easily have taken our foot off the pedal, but we carried on giving our best until the last kick. The night we beat Havant and Waterlooville 2-0 and to win promotion was something so special – to see the crowd on the edge of the pitch from the shed wave like and the whole of that evening can still make me emotional. The whole squad bought into the extra training sessions and we also picked up on the educational and scientific side of it watching videos and so on. The club were stronger behind the scenes with the board pulling together and everything clicked on the field – the players were all on it and I told them, 'You do this and get promotion and you will never be forgotten and you may never get the chance to make names for yourselves like this again.'

So, after twenty-one years, County were once more kicking off in the Conference. It had been a long and difficult road back and football likes to throw up storylines, with the first game being at Darlington where County had played their last ever League game. They lost 1-0 but quickly showed the ability to compete at this level. Dreams of a second successive promotion were not looking fanciful, even topping the League for a brief time. County may well have reached the play-offs, but the end of 2010 brought the shattering news that Holdsworth was leaving for Aldershot, and with him went the belief and desire of many of the side and all hopes of that ultimate League return. Just as bad was the sale of prolific Craig Reid in the January transfer window. Tim Harris had returned as director of football when Holdsworth's revolving door was spinning and his knowledge of this level of football and ability to work with the board had undoubtedly played a major part in the previous season's success. The board turned to him, not wanting to be rushed into a decision – and results were simply awful as the squad suffered a major hangover. Harris told me,

> Being caretaker manager it was totally different – an absolute nightmare! A League club had been in for Dean and I'd spoken to him and said they were not the right club for him and he needed to be patient – he wouldn't have been given time there and their record since with managers bears that out. To be fair, he listened, but then literally a couple of months later he said he was going to Aldershot. I think in that period he felt that he'd taken us as far as he could. A number of key players had tremendous loyalty to Dean – they were besotted with him, and to be honest they found it very very difficult to adjust to life without him when he left. One of our best players said to me, 'Can I be honest with you – my head's gone!' In the end, Anthony Hudson was appointed and we got a few improved results.

Hudson, son of the legendary Alan, came recommended by the likes of Harry Redknapp and was absurdly touted as the new Mourinho. However, he was very young, had no playing pedigree whatsoever and, despite his coaching badges, no management experience at anywhere near this level. Appointed on April Fools' day, he initially quietened his doubters and had some impressive results, including a 7-1 win at Gateshead, who were left in no doubt by the many visitors in fancy dress that Newport was most certainly Welsh, and proud of it! Despite the dreadful spell under Harris, County finished a very respectable ninth, just nine points short of the play-offs. What may have been had Holdsworth not left, or at least the side shown greater resolve?

Hudson's doubters were soon able to say 'told you so' as clearly looking out of his depth he was sacked before the end of September! Six days later, the board made the inspired appointment of ex-Spurs star Justin Edinburgh. Chris Blight told me,

What happened with Hudson, even with my limited experience, I could see wasn't going to work in a month of Sundays. I think the result at Mansfield when we lost 5-0 was the final nail in the coffin that meant he had to go regardless of the financial consequences. I had been tailing Justin for months as when I was on the Conference board one of his Director's at Rushden spoke to me privately saying, 'You want to look at this guy.' Lots of clubs wanted him and I was thrilled to bits we got him. We looked at all of the applications and his was like a cork coming to the surface.

Edinburgh made some astute additions, including Lee Minshull, Andy Sandell and on loan young Nottingham Forest 'keeper, Karl Darlow, who made a big impression. Admission to the Welsh Cup had been permitted for the first time since 1992, but ended ludicrously when County were forced to play their tie at TNS on the same day as a League game! Safety was secured with three games remaining, but the final game of the season was a historic occasion – as County played at Wembley for the first time ever! There were emotional scenes at Wealdstone when County survived the second leg of the semi-final of the FA Trophy. Over 12,000 amber-clad fans were determined to enjoy their day out at the home of football whatever the result. Darlow was not allowed to play, but the game may have ended differently had Romone Rose scored an early one-on-one opportunity. York changed their game plan in the second half and won 2-0, but for many they were disappointed but just happy to be there. I will always recall a York fan coming up to me after the game and saying, 'Don't worry, you will be back here again next season and go up!' As if!

And so County entered their centenary season with hopes that in Edinburgh they had a man who could at least consolidate Conference status. While formed with the express purpose of one day returning League football to Newport, there had been a feeling among many that if the Conference was the pinnacle, at least the club had been returned from where it had fallen from grace. With automatic promotion to the League now effectively making it the Fifth Division, the fixture list was full of memories, with many old foes from the Football League days now featured. A move of enormous importance was announced before a ball was even kicked as County moved home to Rodney Parade. How ironic would it be, having been formed 100 years before as an alternative to the other code, if County could achieve its greatest success at the home of Newport rugby? Edinburgh was in no doubt that in terms of attracting the right quality of player and setting the team up in the way he wanted to win games and entertain the crowd would mean moving from Spytty, commenting, 'If the club is going to evolve and grow and get back into the Football League then it is essential we move.' Director Howard Greenhaf told me,

The season we nearly got relegated, the pitch was in a terrible state. Chris Blight had been invited to something over at Rodney Parade and he came back saying it was brilliant and then I was invited and came back saying, 'Chris, we have got to go there!' We bumped into Martyn Hazell and said how fantastic it was, and after a time they agreed to look at our interest in coming to an arrangement with them. In the middle of all of that, a floodlight collapsed when changing a bulb. It could have killed someone! The ground was closed and we took the opportunity again to speak to them and raised the possibility of a temporary move. We agreed to play our last five home games at Rodney Parade and we even bought goalposts, but the council put in temporary lights and the Conference said that in fairness to the competition we had to stay and play at Spytty. The terracing had also been condemned as it did not comply with the stadia regs, and so we also needed to replace the Shed terraces, etc. The council was clearly not going to sort the pitch. Temporary seating arrangements were also expensive for putting up and taking down – there was so much stuff that had to be done – probably between 50 and 100 grand just to play at Conference level – and if we were going to make any progress we needed to look elsewhere. We had a meeting with supporters groups over at Rodney Parade and went around the stadium, making it clear it was their decision as much as the board's, and it was amazing how the visit changed reactions and they voted for it, which was brilliant. But there was still a huge amount to be done to be able to accommodate everyone's requirements and do the deal!

To be successful there is little room for sentiment and so it was to be thank you and goodbye to many of the squad. In May, the *Argus* had reflected,

An upwardly mobile squad of winners playing at the magnificent Rodney Parade with a style and swagger, or a hastily assembled group of long ball merchants clogging it around Spytty Park? The answer is probably neither, the truth in between, but this will be quite the summer for Newport County fans.

Well it turned into quite a summer, winter and spring, and swagger and style at Rodney Parade was the order of the day. Inevitably, the move to a new home was not without its difficulty. The famous old posts that had seen the All Blacks beaten in 1963 were far too heavy to be moved so frequently and that was but one of the logistical issues that needed to be resolved. Pontypool RFC were also fighting a High Court case to stay in the Welsh Premiership, and this could put a spanner in the works by delaying fixtures being settled. This was a potentially enormous obstacle because of the Conference's requirement for football fixtures to be given precedence. If left too late, then the logistics (with the best will in the world) would surely have been too complex. Would the High Court indirectly turn from friend to foe in County's history? On 31 May, a three-year contract was signed and there was a fond farewell to Spytty, although Newport council were helpful in keeping the door open to return should things not work out. Gary Warren left for Inverness, but fiery ex-Welsh international David Pipe was a ready-made replacement as captain. July, however, was a less than glorious period in the 100 years, as the power of the internet was felt in full force with abusive criticism of the board (and Chairman Blight in particular) in the light of a rumoured consortium's offer being ignored. After ten years in which Blight had given heart and soul to the role, he understandably considered the impact and intrusion unacceptable and resigned. David Hando stepped into the breach temporarily. Bristol Rovers were the first to appear at the new home, and County won the pre-season game 2-0 with new signing Jefferson Lewis scoring the historic first goal. Then on 3 July, the *Argus* carried a headline that could have made all the difference in 1989: 'County Role for Lotto Millionaire'! £45 million Euro Lottery winner Les Scadding had caught the bug as a board guest the previous year and agreed to join. He was clear he would be no sugar daddy, but explained, 'Because of the regrettable situation with Chris and the fact the club has been left with only one director, it seems right to come on now officially.'

Scadding made his way to the away end after the final whistle of the first League game at promotion favourites Mansfield. Memories of Hudson's 5-0 drubbing had been wiped away with a sensational 4-3 win. Debutants

included 'keeper Lenny Pidgeley, a late replacement for the injured new No.
1 Alan Julian, centre-back Tony James, who netted the goal of the game, and
effervescent new striker Aaron O'Connor, who also scored. The first home
League encounter at Rodney Parade soon followed and 2,646 saw Nuneaton
sent packing 4-0, O'Connor scoring the first. The form continued and prior
to the Braintree game, where County came from behind to win 2-1, Scadding
was announced as chairman. Next was the greatly anticipated game home
to old rivals Hereford and a 2-0 win, featuring a sensational strike from
Sandell, saw County astonishingly complete the first month with a 100 per
cent record from five games.

I was given the privilege of compering the Centenary Dinner at the Celtic
Manor on 27 October. Attended by 600 guests, including the current squad
and sixty former players and managers, I concluded with the toast, 'Newport
County AFC – the next 100 years!' and, having outlined our dramatic history,
pointed out to the current stars that they had the opportunity to make their
names legendary for generations to come. County had disappointingly lost that
day, but nevertheless were top of the League. Inducted into the Hall of Fame
that evening were Len Weare, sadly a posthumous award, having passed away
suddenly in September, Keith Oakes, Mark Price, Nathan Davies, Craig Reid and
kit man Tony Gilbert, in recognition of his thirty-seven years of service. They
joined existing inductees Tommy Tynan, Albert Derrick Snr, David Williams,
Ken Morgan, John Relish, Roddy Jones, Kevin Moore and Chris Lilygreen.

It seemed that every time County had a blip, so did their promotion rivals.
A major addition was made to the side, with the loan signing in December of
Wimbledon's Christian Jolley, who made an immediate impact, scoring five
in as many games before being recalled. When Christmas was over, County
were second, just a point behind Grimsby and with a game in hand, but still
few outside of Newport felt they would last the course. The transfer window
was dominated by the 'will he won't he' signing of Jolley; County kept their
nerve and eventually got their man. Unfortunately, the window closed, with
the inevitable sale to Wolves of teenage youth product Lee Evans, who had
sensationally made his debut at Wembley. There were genuine worries that a
fixture pile up would derail the promotion challenge, with County needing to fit
in fifteen games in fifty days. The game at Gateshead, who had pitch problems,
reached preposterous proportions, eventually being played at Boston. From
mid-March, County went on a nine-game unbeaten run. A change of formation
saw new signing Byron Anthony particularly impressive in defence, and the
sequence was only ended at Grimsby as Edinburgh rested five of his side after

the play-offs had already been secured. County had finished third and indeed it was to be a return to Grimsby for the first leg as they finished fourth.

'Time to end the exile,' declared Edinburgh travelling to the game the day before to prepare in earnest. 'We've travelled quickly in a short space of time and maybe they've had a longer time building the squad at Grimsby, but I don't think that matters. Now we're in it to win it.' I attended the first leg at Grimsby with Keith Oakes and we reflected on the huge significance of the ninety minutes ahead. Make no mistake, Keith was experiencing the same nervous excitement as any County diehard – this was no ordinary game. County started sharply, with Jolley running his heart out alongside Crow, who played in place of the not quite fit O'Connor. Eighteen-year-old loanee Alex Gilbey was also starting, and he justified his selection with an outstanding performance. The second half was more uncomfortable as Grimsby started the brighter. The game took on a continental appearance as a flare was thrown on the pitch, much to the annoyance of County fans, who hardly needed Pidgeley's job trying to keep the threatening Grimsby attack at bay being made more difficult by one of their own. On seventy-seven minutes, Grimsby hit the upright from only a couple of yards out and, with just four minutes remaining, Pidgeley again performed heroics. Hearing the whistle and a draw to take back to Newport at that point would have been met with great relief. Just two minutes later, forget relief – it was all about jubilant celebration! Jolley was fouled and had to retire from play, but Sandell's free kick (not for the first time in the season) was met by Ismail Yakubu and, having been denied twice in the first half, he was not about to spurn another. His downward header found the net with it being unclear to all at the other end of the pitch if it had come off a defender en route. Who cared? It was 1-0 and Sunday could not come quick enough! As we left the ground to find my car in a Cleethorpes side street to make our comparatively quick journey back home to Lincoln, I gazed in wonderment at the County coaches lined up with slightly disbelieving expressions on the faces of so many familiar County players. A large sign outside the ground advertised that night's game and I turned to Keith and, trying to choke back my emotion, said, 'I thought I'd lost these days for good.' Keith, that rock of our greatest conquests, simply smiled and said, 'Get used to it Andrew mate – I think you are going to enjoy a lot more of these.'

How nail-biting would the next few days be? A draw would be enough, but David Pipe wanted to take no chances: 'We won't try and defend the one goal lead, that's not how we play our best football. My advice will be to approach it as if its 0-0. Its half-time in the game, nothing is achieved.' Former youth product Mike Flynn, who had gone on to play in the Championship, had been the marquee summer signing but said, 'This is the game I've looked forward to most in my career. I've played a lot of big games but this one means the most to me. As a Newport boy I know how much it would mean for this club and this city to get into League 2.' The front page of the *Argus* on Monday 29 April declared '90 MINUTES FROM HISTORY'. The Exiles were on their way to Wembley – again!

Grimsby came to town and, big and direct, they gave their all. With County looking nervous in front of a crowd of 6,616, there were some anxious moments in the first half, none more so than when the brilliant Pidgeley dived full length low to his left to heart-stoppingly prevent the visitors levelling the all important aggregate score. Had that gone in, maybe history would be taking a different course, but this team was not for laying down – there was too much at stake. Every player and supporter had completely bought into the 'mission' started by David Hando and company in 1989. County slowly awoke from their slumber, with Gilbey beginning to exert his influence, and it was the youngster who supplied Jolley who took one touch before shooting into the corner for 2-0 on aggregate. In the second half, the confidence level rose noticeably, and although this was Newport County AFC, the result seemed in little doubt. The only scare was when, with moments remaining, Pidgeley inexplicably handled the ball just outside his area. He thankfully escaped with a yellow card and not a red. We really were on our way to Wembley!

Edinburgh declared, 'It was an ultimate team display – I am so proud of the players. This eclipses getting to the trophy final last season. A lot of people deserve credit and chairman Les Scadding is definitely one of them, because without him Christian Jolley wouldn't even be here.' Jolley, who had been born five days after County's last ever League game, was already looking forward to his day out, as he was determined to reach a target he had set himself earlier in the season: 'My target was fifteen goals when I came here and I'm on fourteen now so a goal at Wembley would put me where I want to be!' His eyes were on the bigger prize of course: 'We're not going to stop here – we are going to finish the job we started he added. We want to end the season with a party.' And Edinburgh was doubly determined to do it for the fans: 'The fans have been the main reason I've stayed at the football club, they are magnificent, they didn't let their nerves creep onto the pitch and all credit to them.' County would face Wrexham in an all-Welsh Final.

10

MISSION ACCOMPLISHED

This time going to Wembley was far less about the occasion – it was all about the result. The media frenzy inevitably focussed on the early struggles as the fledgling Newport AFC. This was the most implausible and romantic of stories. Among the many supporters being interviewed daily was original director Colin Jones. Given his past contribution, it was not a surprise that he would be at Wembley – other than he would be making a 21,000 mile round trip from his home in Sydney! Colin was not alone in making the trip from down under but he would arrive on the morning of the game and return the same evening! County fans really are the most devoted exiles! Canada and other far flung corners would also see amber-clad passengers at booking-in desks.

We all have our memories of that day. I spoke to supporters who were full of confidence and those like me who had experienced too much to tempt fate by demonstrating any sense of bravado. It was tense and it was emotional. It was unspeakably thrilling and the anticipation was tangible. Thoughts of full time brought visions of utter despair or the greatest sense of achievement imaginable. Is that an exaggeration? Not if you have been riding the County roller coaster all these years! When arriving at Wembley I had just left my car when my mobile rang with a message alert. It was a text from my first ever favourite County player, Jeff Thomas, who could not be there but was wishing us luck. In the concourse, I was bear-hugged from behind by Norman Parselle, our first ever goalscorer in those now distant days at Moreton. My heart was pounding and it was hard to strike a conversation. I have never wanted a day to go so fast! We all of us there had our memories and our hopes, and hopefully many were able to enjoy the build up (and indeed much of the game) more than I did! David Hando spoke of the past, remembering, 'We weren't dreamers, it was a mission and now we are ninety minutes away from making it mission accomplished.'

Bringing the story up to date, Chairman Les Scadding declared,

> I know some people think I'm mad to invest funds into a football club because we all know it's the easiest way to lose money, but I really enjoy my association with the County. People say the club is being run by a lottery winner and a builder and in response to that I say that is so true, but look at what we've done! People have no concept of what Howard Greenhaf has done for the club, he's done an amazing amount to get us to Rodney Parade, and we wouldn't be here now without him.

Justin Edinburgh added,

> Our expectations for the season were not success to this extent – we just didn't see potential promotion coming this quickly. At the start of the season I tipped Mansfield Kidderminster, Luton, Grimsby and Wrexham as likely title challengers and my outside hope was that, just maybe, we could sneak the play-offs.

Edinburgh also revealed that the preparations would be toned down compared to the previous season's visit:

> In a way it is good that the players are like they are, living in their own world some of them not really considering how big the game is. It can be dangerous. Take Sam Foley last year in the FA Trophy final and it's no criticism of Sam but leading up to the final he had been the player who inspired us, but in the Final he had his worst game for months. We burdened him a lot. He and Gary Warren were up in Wembley for a press day and then we went up for two days before and had a look around the stadium. This time we do it differently, we approach it as a normal away game with an overnight stay.

County lined up with Pidgeley in goal, Pipe and Sandell in the wing back positions, and with Yakubu flanked in defence by James and Anthony. Gilbey deservedly held his place in midfield alongside Minshull and Flynn, who was relishing his premonition months earlier that County would win promotion by beating Wrexham at Wembley and Jolley and Crow up front. Injury-hit top scorer O'Connor was a potential match-winning substitute on the bench with Donnelly, Hughes, Willmott and Julian. Never has 'Mae Hen Wlad Fy Nhadau' been sung more proudly as Wembley was turned into Little Wales – 'God Save the Queen' was a little less enthusiastically observed! The game was being played out as could be expected – tense, nervous, tentative exchanges with the price of a mistake being beyond contemplation. County's first foray of any description occurred on five minutes, when Jolley caught full-back Neil Ashton in possession and sent a ball across the edge of the box that Flynn drove straight at 'keeper Chris Maxwell.

Wrexham edged the early encounters, with Brett Ormerod hitting the side netting on sixteen minutes. He missed again when well placed on thirty-seven minutes and came closer just a minute later. That kick-started County and a Minshull header was well held by Maxwell on forty-one minutes and Crow teed-up Jolley, who missed the angle of post and bar by inches with one of his trademark curlers. Half-time arrived goalless with one moment of inspiration or carelessness potentially deciding the outcome. At least the closing exchanges gave hope and no doubt Edinburgh was already choosing his words carefully for the most important forty-five minutes ever.

With Pipe and Sandell settling and offering their usual outlets, County looked more competitive after the break and a decent opportunity arrived on forty-nine minutes. Jolley ghosted past Stephen Wright down the left, before crossing for Crow, who nodded his attempt straight at a relieved Maxwell. Wrexham responded and a brace of corners failed to pierce County's resistance. The clearest opening of the game arrived on fifty-eight minutes; striker Ormerod, one of the most experienced players on the pitch, was once again well placed, but spurned a gilt-edged chance that can now be looked at as one of the games most important moments. Pipe rampaged down the right on sixty minutes, his ball finding Flynn who subsequently picked out Jolley at the far post; sadly, his close-range attempt was stabbed wide of the mark. Edinburgh decided that fresh blood was needed and Wrexham's nerves could not have been helped by the sight of the lethal O'Connor coming on for Crow on sixty-two minutes. The ever-dangerous Jolley almost burst clear on eighty-four minutes, only an exceptional last-ditch challenge from Martin Riley sparing Wrexham. With extra time looming and supporters looking anxiously to see who was showing signs of fatigue, it was to prove a clear warning that ultimately wasn't heeded; within two more minutes, Jolley had raced clear once more and this time there would be no respite for the shattered Wrexham side. A long, probing ball from Sandell cleared the head of defender Artell and Jolley was away like a greyhound and onside. What happened next will be forever etched in County folklore, the striker showing wonderful composure to lift the ball over the on-rushing Maxwell and into the back of the net. The amber-coloured part of Wembley simply erupted – County were now just four minutes (plus change) away from the Football League! As a true personal recollection of that moment, as the ball hit the net in slow motion, I searched first for the referee and then his assistant, fearing a flag or simply any reason to deny us. This was then met with not only my scream, but an audible ping in my left temporal lobe and an instant mother of headaches! I instantly thought, 'Typical Newport County, we are going to do it at last – and I'm going to have a stroke and miss it!' My son Sean turned to me and asked if I was okay – and then the tears flowed – and kept flowing for most of the next hour! I was not alone!

In the meantime, celebrations turned to yet more nerves as Wrexham piled on the pressure in search of a desperate equaliser to take it to extra time. The stunned Dragons threw on striker Dele Adebola and added yet another forward to their now massed ranks as goalkeeper Maxwell made his way to the other end. Two corners were won, the frantic 'keeper showing little sign now of wanting to return to his goal as not only the kitchen sink was thrown at the Exiles, but the dirty dishes and the Fairy Liquid as well! Pidgeley had been outstanding all afternoon and he would need to be in these closing moments as five minutes of stoppage time had been agonisingly signalled. There was only a minute left when one corner too many saw a header that, from my vantage point, looked destined for the top of the opposite side of the net from where Pidgeley appeared rooted. Somehow he glided elegantly across goal and not only saved but held the effort. Just keep possession! Instead, Sandell cleared and found Jolley in the sort of position from which you always felt he could manufacture something special. He moved towards goal before squaring unselfishly to O'Connor, whose shot was saved, but rebounded to him and he was the calmest man in the ground as he adjusted his position to supremely execute a volley that brought the house down as it bulged the net. With his shirt off as he ran to the County faithful behind the goal, leaving the Wrexham players on their knees, the aftermath will remain in the consciousness forever as ecstatic scenes bordering on sheer insanity ensued: grown men, women and children weeping with joy, strangers hugging what little breath remained out of each other, while the County bench seemed to multiply in numbers as they left their vantage point to join in the celebrations. Wrexham kicked off and two seconds later the whistle blew and we were back.

Readers of this book may feel that County's history seems just a little too far-fetched to be true. And there we were at Wembley with the final kick of the final game of our centenary season, clinching promotion back to the League after twenty-five years, twenty-four years after going out of existence. You really could not make it up. Fittingly, just 2 minutes later, I received another text. This time it was from the great Keith Oakes, saying, 'Congrats to all at the club,' and two minutes later another from Keith, saying, 'Fantastic, so pleased!' Seeing Pipe and his teammates lifting the play-off trophy and the post-match scenes on the pitch with Justin Edinburgh thrown skywards, words can't do them justice.

As the trophy was passed around the Royal Box, the biggest cheer was deservedly reserved for Justin Edinburgh. John Relish, of course, was there, and told me, 'Now they are back in the League it revalidates the CV of the old players like me and I am not the only one to think that – people now recognise that we played for a League club! So Justin's done a job for all of us too!'

Supporters' Club president Cath Clarke said, 'I maintain that apart from the High Court victory, 5 May 2013 will go on record as the most important date in County history.'

'I feel incredibly emotional,' explained the proud Edinburgh afterwards. 'This club has been to hell and back; we are a family club and so many people give time and effort and I'm so happy for them. We have incredibly special fans and this is a present for them.'

Striker Christian Jolley added,

It's an epic story and I'm so happy to be a part of it; we were nervous first half because we knew how much it meant to the fans and to us players as well. There was so much at stake and it was a lot to take in, but we settled down after the break and ended up on top. Lenny Pidgeley was absolutely superb; he dominated them and they couldn't get anything past him. The Gaffer said to us to make sure you give everything you've got and we did that; it was a great, great day.

Jolley also explained his choice of gloves on a warm afternoon: 'The gloves were a bit of a superstition really. The lads gave me a bit of stick for wearing them but I've done all right in them so I kept them on and it worked! I didn't want to change anything.'

Aaron O'Connor, who had capped off a wonderful season in the best possible style despite his injury frustration, commented,

My body is still shaking! It was tough to start on the bench but the team has played so well in the play-offs and they deserved to start. But for me to come on and score was unbelievable, I didn't know what to do. I took my shirt off and got booked but I don't care. I went mad and it's the perfect end to the season for me and for the team.

Inspirational captain David Pipe reflected that he had not only repaid the debt that he owed the club for rescuing his career but had justified his belief by turning down offers to move to League clubs during the summer:

Football can be a horrible place sometimes and I know the dark times can be very dark, but this is an amazing feeling. Newport put their hand out to help me. I grabbed it and I've never let go and I won't be letting go. What the Gaffer has done in a very short space of time is nothing short of a miracle. I told them to take the lid off the trophy when they presented it because I knew I was going to drop it. I was emotionally drained and it felt very heavy, but it felt fantastic.

Man of the match Lenny Pidgeley had endured heartbreak in his previous visits to Wembley and after a spell out of the side had returned in sensational form, conceding only four goals in the final twelve games and clean sheets in the play offs. He beamed as he said,

I've never enjoyed myself at Wembley and to play and win now is brilliant. It's not normally the goalkeeper who gets man of the match so I'll take that, definitely – it's about time we got some plaudits! I was a bit hurt in the second half, but we still managed to keep them out thanks to our defence. I would have been a bit lost if someone had put it across the box but our defenders made sure that never happened.

Andy Sandell revealed that the day had been a blur and admitted that he had taken inspiration from an unlikely source:

When I got up in the morning the first song I heard on the radio was Martine McCutcheon singing 'This Is My Moment' and I thought, alright, I hope so, that's a good omen! Then I got to Wembley and I had the same dressing room and the same locker as when I won the play-off final at Wembley with Bristol Rovers. I just looked at Byron Anthony, a teammate at Rovers, and we were both thinking, 'Yes, this has to be a good sign for us.' As for the assist, I can't really remember it, everyone swamped me and I've been told several times I got the assist for the goal, but I honestly don't remember it!

Finally, Edinburgh, who as a player had graced the Premiership with Spurs, confessed the full extent of the personal meaning to him from his relatively short time in Wales.

I was lucky enough to play top level but I think you lose association with fans and people. Coming to non-league is the best thing I ever did because I fell back in love with the game. There are a lot of volunteers at this club who give up their time and effort for no money – this is payback for them. It's been tough for them to see their city lose its football club; I was involved with Rushden and I think those at levels above don't understand what impact it has on the community when that happens. I'm giving back something to all the people who worked tirelessly before me. We have special fans; this was a present for them. It took coming to non-league football to make me appreciate things. In the bubble at the top you lose sight of what made you love the game as a kid. Coming to Newport has rekindled that for me.

The day after Wembley, I received a text from the man whose leadership saw us through the darkest days – David Hando, now club president. It simply said, 'Mission Accomplished!'

The centenary season ended in rare celebratory style on an open-top bus. What can the next 100 years possibly throw up to match the first? We all pray not two world wars and bankruptcy! It has been a roller coaster of epic proportions, and thoughts are with those who were not there to see the thrilling conclusion. People like Bert Moss and Alderman Wardle, whose dedication saw us through the most desperate of times, not just for club but for country; Jimmy Hindmarsh and Billy Lucas, whose wheeling and dealing literally kept us in the game; Ray Wilcox, Len Weare and Keith Saunders, who gave us a lifetime of service; and the countless supporters who had amber in the blood and who were no doubt in the thoughts of so many at Wembley. The shirt in its various shades has been worn by players for whom the title 'legend' seems barely sufficient and whose deeds will never be allowed to diminish, but final reflections are with the gloriously defiant David Hando and John Relish-led 'exiles', who refused to accept logic, and the current board, management team and squad, who ultimately proved the doubters wrong and gave us the ultimate season of triumph. We salute you all and await with the next chapter with eager anticipation!

ABOUT THE AUTHOR

Andrew Taylor, is the club historian for Newport County AFC, the author of *Look Back in Amber: Memories of Newport County AFC* and *Mission Accomplished: The Ultimate Season of Triumph* and wrote in the club's programme for ten years. He is also secretary of the Newport County AFC Former Players' Association. Married with two children, Sean and Lauren, and two grandchildren, Rhiannon and Jasmine, Andrew retired from his position of Chief Executive of the City of Lincoln Council, in which he is the second-longest serving member since 1910. He has been installed with the honour of being made an 'Honorary Freeman of the City'. In October 2015, before a County home game against Portsmouth, Andrew was inducted as the twenty-third member of the 'Newport County Hall of Fame'.

The author pictured with his son, Sean, at Wembley when County got back into the League.

Club legend John Relish, to Andrew's surprise, formally inducting him into the 'Hall of Fame' prior to the game against Portsmouth in October 2015.

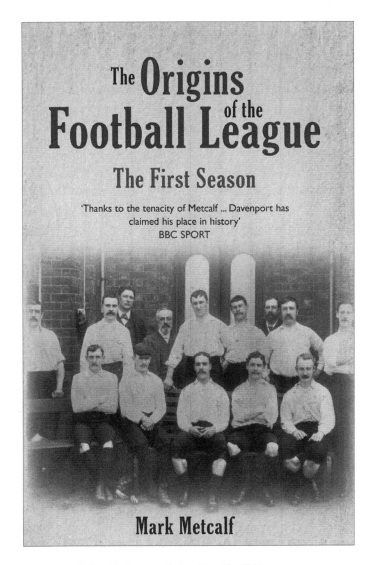

The Origins of the Football League

The First Season

'Thanks to the tenacity of Metcalf ... Davenport has claimed his place in history'
BBC SPORT

Mark Metcalf

The Origins of the Football League
Mark Metcalf

A fascinating insight the formation of the Football League, including the discovery of who really scored the first ever League goal.

978 1 4456 4017 4

288 pages